The Roman Catholic Bishops of Hexham and Newcastle

— PAUL SEVERN —

Sacristy
Press

Sacristy Press
PO Box 612, Durham, DH1 9HT

www.sacristy.co.uk

First published in 2022 by Sacristy Press, Durham

Copyright © Paul Severn 2022
The moral rights of the author have been asserted.

All rights reserved, no part of this publication may be reproduced or transmitted in any form or by any means, electronic, mechanical photocopying, documentary, film or in any other format without prior written permission of the publisher.

Every reasonable effort has been made to trace the copyright holders of material reproduced in this book, but if any have been inadvertently overlooked the publisher would be glad to hear from them.

Sacristy Limited, registered in England & Wales, number 7565667

British Library Cataloguing-in-Publication Data
A catalogue record for the book is available from the British Library

ISBN 978-1-78959-210-8

Contents

Introduction 1

1. William Hogarth (1850–66) 9
2. James Chadwick (1866–82) 25
3. John William Bewick (1882–6) 35
4. Henry O'Callaghan (1887–9) 41
5. Thomas William Wilkinson (1889–1909) 51
5A. Richard Preston (1900–4) 59
6. Richard Collins (1909–24) 63
7. Joseph William Thorman (1924–36) 71
8. Joseph McCormack (1937–58) 81
9. James Cunningham (1958–74) 91
10. Hugh Lindsay (1974–92) 97
10A. Owen Francis Swindlehurst (1977–95) 105
11. (John Michael Martin) Ambrose Griffiths (1992–2004) 109
12. Kevin John Dunn (2004–8) 121
13. Séamus Cunningham (2009–19) 129
14. Robert John Byrne (2019–) 139

Epilogue 146
Acknowledgements 149
Bibliography 150

Introduction

It was during the Protestant Reformation, in 1534, that King Henry VIII passed the Act of Supremacy, by which he rejected all foreign laws or foreign authority, particularly papal authority, and declared himself head of the Church in England. The monasteries were suppressed; in time the Latin liturgy was abandoned and replaced by an alternative in the vernacular, and many of the Church's artefacts were seized or destroyed. Although there was a brief respite for Catholics under Queen Mary I, who reigned from 1553 to 1558, her successor, Queen Elizabeth, during her long reign (1558–1603), consolidated the work of her father, King Henry. By establishing the Church of England in 1559, all aspects of Catholic life were effectively outlawed and the penalties for adhering to the "old religion", to its beliefs or practices, were severe: imprisonment, torture and even death.

However, Catholicism in England was never completely eradicated. It continued underground. Recusant families, often based in large rural estates, sheltered heroic priests who travelled incognito from continental Europe. Many of these came from the English College at Douai in Flanders, founded by William Cardinal Allen in 1568. Indeed, it is estimated that some 450 priests had been sent to the English Mission by the end of Elizabeth I's reign in 1603. Whitby was a noted landing place for Catholic missionary priests, and there were a number of cells of Catholicism in the North-East, perhaps most notably the Withams of Cliffe Hall, the Jenisons of Walworth, the Garnetts of Blackwell and the Parkinsons of Whessoe.

A number of Catholic martyrs are also particularly associated with the North-East. A group of four—the Durham martyrs of 1594—was composed of two priests and two laymen. Fr John Boste (b. circa 1543) was educated at Oxford and took Anglican orders, but then travelled to Rheims and was ordained as a Catholic. He returned to England in 1581 and worked in the North, making trips to Scotland too. He was said to be "the most sought-after priest in the north and several attempts were made to capture him".[1] He was eventually captured, on 10 September 1593, at the house of William Claxton at Waterhouses near Brancepeth, Durham. He spent some time in the Tower of London before being tried at Durham Assizes and was executed in Durham on 24 July 1594.

Alongside him was another priest, the Jesuit Fr John Ingram, who was from Herefordshire and also studied at Rheims, where he was ordained. He travelled widely and was for a time chaplain to Sir Walter Lindsay of Balgarvies Castle near Forfar in Scotland, but he was captured at Wark in Northumberland having crossed from Scotland into England at Berwick-upon-Tweed. He similarly spent time in the Tower, where he was tortured. He remained firm and said nothing that might compromise his friends. He stood trial in Durham and was executed in Gateshead on 26 July 1594.

George Swallowell was an Anglican cleric, possibly born in Darlington, who converted to Catholicism. He was arrested in 1593 for his work in "reconciling subjects to Rome" and, after his trial alongside the two priests, was executed in Darlington marketplace on 26 July 1594. Also included in this group of four was John Speed, who was arrested for offering assistance to priests and declined invitations to recant his Catholicism. He was executed in Durham on 4 February 1594. All four were among the eighty-five martyrs of England, Scotland and Wales beatified by Pope Pius XI in 1929. Boste was canonized by Pope Paul VI in 1970 as one of the Forty Martyrs of England and Wales.

Other notable martyrs associated with the North-East include Blessed Thomas Plumtree. He studied in Oxford and became rector of Stubton in his native Lincolnshire. He resigned his living at the accession of Queen Elizabeth I rather than take the oaths required of him and travelled north to become chaplain to Thomas Percy, Earl of Northumberland, who was the leader of the 1569 uprising in the North. He is particularly noted for celebrating a Mass at Durham Cathedral on 4 December 1569 at which clergy and people who had conformed to the new religion were reconciled to the old faith. Plumtree is described as "preacher to the rebels". Recriminations followed the collapse of this revolt and Plumtree was executed on 4 January 1570. His master, Earl Percy, was executed two years later on 26 August 1572. Both were beatified by Pope Leo XIII in 1896.

Blessed John Storey MP has little connection with the North-East beyond his birth in Northumberland in 1504. He was an Oxford-educated lawyer, who became Oxford's first Regius Professor of Civil Law and principal of Broadgates Hall, now Pembroke College. He rose to high office, then escaped abroad, but during a search for contraband and heretical books on a ship harboured in Antwerp, the ship's hatches were closed with Storey on board, and the ship returned to England. Storey was arrested and subsequently executed at Tyburn in 1571.

Blessed James Layburne was born in Lincolnshire and studied at Corpus Christi College, Oxford, but took part in an uprising of northern Catholics against Queen Elizabeth I. When the uprising failed, he was captured. He was offered his freedom if he abjured the faith, which he refused. He was hanged in Durham in 1583.

It was towards the end of the eighteenth century, under King George III, that the harsh anti-Catholic penal laws started to be dismantled. The First Catholic Relief Act, known as the Papists Act, was passed in 1778 and, although it did not grant freedom for worship, it allowed Catholics to join the army and purchase land if they took an oath of allegiance. The Second Relief Act of 1791 was more far-reaching than the Papists Act and (loosely) permitted the building of Catholic churches (albeit without steeples or bells) and the exercise of the Catholic religion. In 1829, the Third Catholic Relief Act (the Catholic Emancipation Act) marked the conclusion of the reforms. It repealed the Test Act of 1672 and the remaining penal laws. Catholics were once again allowed to take an active part in the civic and political life of a borough and the state, and were again allowed to sit in Parliament at Westminster.

These pieces of legislation are important for they paved the way for Pope Pius IX to promulgate the Bull, *Universalis Ecclesiae*, on 29 September 1850, by which the Catholic hierarchy in England and Wales was restored. (The Scottish hierarchy was not restored until 4 March 1878, when Pope Leo XIII promulgated *Ex Supremo Apostolatus Apice*.) The London Vicariate (one of eight), previously administered by an apostolic vicar, became the Metropolitan Archdiocese of Westminster, and there were a further twelve dioceses covering England and Wales.

One of these was the diocese of Hexham, one of the original suffragan sees within the province of Westminster. We may also observe that Hexham was a truly ancient diocese. The ancient diocese of York was divided in 678 by Archbishop Theodore of Canterbury, forming a bishopric between the Rivers Aln and Tees with the seat at Hexham. Eleven bishops followed St Eata, who was bishop from 678 until c. 681, and six of these were saints. After the death of Bishop Tidfrith, the eighth of Hexham, the see was merged with the ancient see of Lindisfarne, which was eventually transferred to Durham at the end of the tenth century. Following the re-establishment of the diocese of Hexham in 1850, the Church of St Mary at Newcastle was designated as the cathedral.

The cathedral in Newcastle was established by Fr (and later Bishop) William Riddell, who was William Hogarth's predecessor as Vicar Apostolic of the Northern District. Riddell was born in 1807 and educated at Stonyhurst. He studied for the priesthood at the Venerable English College in Rome and was ordained priest in 1830. For a time, he remained in Rome, acting as secretary to Cardinal Weld. In 1832, he returned to Britain and went to the mission in Newcastle, at first assisting, and subsequently succeeding, Fr Worswick. Brady records Riddell "was greatly distinguished by his zeal in this mission".[2]

One of his acts was to build a new church, funded by halfpenny subscriptions from the community of immigrant workers on Tyneside. Designed by Augustus Welby Pugin, the church was built between 1842 and 1844 in the Gothic Revival style and dedicated to St Mary. There is notable stained glass by William Wailes, and a tower and steeple were added in 1872 following a bequest from the estate of Elizabeth Dunn. The cathedral was extensively renovated in the first decade of the twenty-first century, and a new three-manual organ by Kenneth Tickell, with forty-six stops, was installed in 2013.

In 1844, Riddell was ordained a bishop, titular of Lagania and coadjutor to Bishop Briggs, Apostolic Vicar of the Northern District. When Briggs died in 1847, Riddell succeeded him, but he was only in office for a matter of months before he died too. Riddell, in turn, was succeeded by Bishop Hogarth (see below). When the hierarchy was restored in 1850, St Mary's Church, Newcastle, was raised to the rank of cathedral, for the new diocese of Hexham. In 1860, the dedication of the church was changed to Our Lady of the Assumption, and in 1861, when the diocese of Hexham became the diocese of Hexham and Newcastle, the renamed cathedral became the cathedral for the new see.

By Apostolic Decree (*Decretum de propagande fide*) of Blessed Pope Pius IX, dated 23 May 1861, the diocese of Hexham was renamed Hexham and Newcastle (*Diocesis Hagulstadensis et Novocastrensis*). By Letters Apostolic (*si qua est*) of Pope Pius X, the province of Westminster, covering all of England and Wales, was split into three new provinces: Westminster, Birmingham and Liverpool. Hexham and Newcastle diocese became a constituent part of the Liverpool province. In 1924, Pope Pius XI separated off part of the diocese of Hexham and Newcastle to form the diocese of Lancaster. Hexham and Newcastle today includes the counties of Northumberland and Durham and the unitary authorities of Newcastle upon Tyne, Darlington, Gateshead, Hartlepool, North Tyneside, South Tyneside and Stockton-on-Tees (north of the river).

The diocese covers a total area of some 8,500 square kilometres. At the time of writing, in 2021, the diocese is made up of 149 parishes and there are 194 secular priests under five episcopal vicars.

In addition to the fourteen bishops of Hexham and Newcastle who are the principal subjects of this text, there have been a number of auxiliary bishops in the diocese. Most of these were translated to the see and will be dealt with as such. Two more, Bishop Preston and Bishop Swindlehurst, did not become Bishop of Hexham and Newcastle. The first retired as auxiliary, and the second died in office. To preserve the correspondence between the numbering of the chapters of this text and the order of the bishops, these two auxiliaries will be treated along with the ordinaries under whom they served.

Finally, it is fitting to mention, at least in passing, the heritage of the local saints who established and built up Christianity in the North-East and have left such a powerful and enduring legacy in the area. St Oswald (d. 642) was King of Northumbria, with his headquarters at Bamburgh Castle. While exiled from his kingdom, he was converted to Christianity by the monks on Iona, and when his kingdom was restored, following a battle at Rowley Burn in 634, Oswald set about establishing Christianity in his territory. He invited monks from Iona to establish a monastery at Lindisfarne and evangelize the region.

It was St Aidan (d. 651), an austere monk of Irish or Scottish origin, who established the monastery on Lindisfarne under the rule of St Columba and was, in 635, ordained Bishop of Lindisfarne. Aidan worked closely with Oswald and made numerous missionary journeys from his monastery, establishing and nurturing Christian communities throughout the region. He built churches and founded monasteries, encouraging the monastic way of life. He was noted for his asceticism and gentleness, but described the English, whom he hoped to convert, as "an uncivilized people of an obstinate and barbarous temperament"![3] He was also involved in educating boys, particularly St Oswin, who succeeded St Oswald, and St Chad.

St Cuthbert was born about 634, the son of an affluent family. He became a monk, not at Lindisfarne but at its daughter monastery, Melrose. In due course, Cuthbert became monastic guest-master at Melrose, and subsequently prior, succeeding Prior Boisil, who had nurtured and tutored him. When Eata became abbot of the Lindisfarne monastery, he invited Cuthbert to become prior there, so Cuthbert relocated and set about renewing the Lindisfarne monastery, which had become a little lax. Significantly, he also introduced the Rule of St Benedict there.

After twelve years as prior, Cuthbert retreated to live a more solitary life on an adjoining isle, and thereafter he went to the Farne Islands. Although only a few miles from Lindisfarne, Farne itself is a small, desolate and barren island, standing sheer out of the sea and, as Bede says, "surrounded on all sides by the deep and boundless ocean". Cuthbert built a circular stone shelter, half of which was his chapel and the other half his dwelling, where he could live the life of a hermit, devoted to God.

However, in 684 Cuthbert was elected as Bishop of Hexham. At first he stayed on his island, but in the end Eata, Bishop of Lindisfarne, offered to "swap" with him, and Eata went to Hexham while Cuthbert became Bishop of Lindisfarne. He preached and taught, building up the faith and caring for the poor, while preserving his own simple and frugal way of life. He died in 687, having been a bishop for just a little more than two years, but a monk for thirty-six. The shrine and relics of St Cuthbert are found today in Durham Cathedral.

St Chad (d. 672), mentioned above, gave his name to a Durham college, although he is perhaps more closely associated with the Midlands, which he evangelized. He is the patron of Birmingham Roman Catholic Cathedral and Diocese, and his relics are to be found in Lichfield Cathedral. Chad was educated at Lindisfarne, a pupil of St Aidan. He was a monk and ordained priest and is chiefly remembered for preaching to the Middle Angles, although he travelled widely. He was ordained bishop at an early age and ended up in Lichfield, where he established his see and founded a monastery. He is noted for his wisdom and learning, a holy and devout man, a remarkable teacher.

St Benedict Biscop was born of a noble family in Northumberland; "*nobile quidem stirpe gentis Anglorum*", writes Bede, "*sed non minori nobilitate mentis*" ("of noble lineage among the English, but being no less noble of mind"). He became a monk and spent time abroad at Lérins in southern France. He made a number of visits to Rome before finally returning to his homeland and establishing, in 675, a monastery dedicated to St Peter at Wearmouth—the mouth of the River Wear. Now known as Monkwearmouth, it is on the outskirts of Sunderland. Benedict's monastery was the first stone-built monastery in northern England (the monastery at Lindisfarne was built of wood), and Benedict established a fine library. As well as a hub for evangelization, the monastery became a centre for study and learning of the highest calibre.

It was the considerable library at Wearmouth which enabled St Bede (673–735), a pupil of Abbot Benedict from the age of seven, and later a pupil of Abbot Ceolfrith, to write his magisterial *Ecclesiastical History of the English People*, from which much of the information above ultimately derives. St Bede passed his whole life at the monastery, involved in the daily round of liturgical observance, studying, writing and teaching. He was a keen Latinist, devoted to the Roman observance, which he encouraged in his teaching. He is unique in that he is the only Englishman (or woman!) to have been declared a Doctor of the Church (by Pope Leo XIII in 1899), and he is buried in the Galilee Chapel at the west end of Durham Cathedral.

This potted history is not exhaustive, and is not meant to be, but it gives a flavour of the saints who shaped early Christianity in the North-East, based to a large degree upon monastic observance.

Notes

1. Godfrey Anstruther, *The Seminary Priests*, Vol. I (Gateshead: Northumberland Press, 1968), p. 44.
2. W. M. Brady, *Annals of the Catholic Hierarchy in England and Scotland, AD 1585–1876* (London: John Mozley Stark, 1883), p. 346.
3. From the Venerable Bede and quoted in *Butler's Lives of the Saints*.

1

William Hogarth (1850–66)

After the restoration of the Catholic hierarchy in 1850, William Hogarth, who was Vicar Apostolic for the Northern District, was appointed the first Bishop of Hexham. Eleven years later, that diocese was renamed Hexham and Newcastle, and Hogarth became the first bishop of the renamed diocese. He was born on 25 March 1786, at Dodding Green near Kendal, "where his family had retained their faith and their lands through penal times".[1] With his elder brother Robert (1785–1868), he went to study at Crook Hall and then to Ushaw College, just four miles west of Durham, and was ordained priest, at Ushaw, on 20 December 1809. He would have been one of the very first priests to be ordained there.

William Cardinal Allen founded the English College at Douai in 1568, to continue to train Englishmen for the priesthood during penal times. Many of these ordained men subsequently returned illegally to England to minister. The work of the English College, Douai was brought to an end by the effects of the French Revolution (1789) and it closed in 1793. Because the Catholic Relief Acts had made conditions for Catholics relatively safe once more, the staff and pupils returned to England, and while some of them joined the students and staff at the Old Hall Green Academy, which subsequently became St Edmund's College, in Ware, Hertfordshire, some of the Douai staff established a new seminary in the North.

At first, in October 1794, the exiles located themselves at Crook Hall, some ten miles from Durham, which was leased from George Baker (the Member of Parliament for Durham City), to whom the building belonged. He was the grandson of the original owner, who had remodelled the house in 1716. In a letter written by Thomas Saul, Crook Hall was described as "a spacious stone building situated in a vale whose adjoining hills are bleak and barren", and he adds, "it has this singularity attending it which few other houses can boast; I mean it has no road to it. We came in a chaise from Durham, amidst the greatest danger of being overturned."[2] Despite the difficulties, this little college flourished and grew. Twenty-eight initial students became fifty-six, and Crook Hall soon became too small (most of the rooms had to serve more than one purpose[3]), so, to cut a long story short, in 1804 Bishop William Gibson, formerly president of the English College in Douai (1781–90) and ordained Titular Bishop of Achantus thereafter, started the building of a new college at Ushaw. The first ground was broken on 23 April 1804.

The oldest part of the college was designed by James Taylor and, only four years after the work started, the original building was complete and the new college opened on 2 August 1808. A chapel designed by Pugin was added in 1847, a library followed, and a new bigger chapel, designed by Dunn and Hansom, was built and completed in 1884. Due to continued expansion, a new east wing was added to accommodate seventy-five further students in the 1960s. From 1968 (until 2011), the college was a constituent part of Durham University. In the last quarter of the twentieth century, student numbers went into rapid decline, and the college closed as a seminary in 2011. Today the chapel and the gardens are a visitor attraction, although part of the college is still used by Durham University, and there is a significant library there too.

The Catholic National Library (formerly the Catholic Central Library) was established in 1912 and moved to Victoria in London in 1922. For many years, it was staffed and financed by the Friars of the Atonement. In 1997, the building in London was sold and the significant collection was in danger of being dismantled. It was housed temporarily at St Michael's Abbey, Farnborough, until 2014, when the collection was relocated again to Durham, and is now cared for by the university's Centre for Catholic Studies, a part of the theology faculty.

To return to Hogarth, he went off to Crook Hall in August 1796, barely ten years old. The regime for one so young was tough. The Crook Hall timetable would have been very similar to the future Ushaw timetable, as both were modelled on the regime at Douai. It is described by Sheridan Gilley: "rising at six, meditation in chapel until 7am, then Mass to 7.30, then study until breakfast at quarter to nine, school from 9.30, dinner at 1.00, study at 3.00, prayer at 7.00 till supper, second prayers at 9.15 and then bed. There were two play days a week."[4] Although very austere by modern standards, and we can imagine the college would have been very cold in the winter, Hogarth and his fellow pupil, and later bishop, George Brown acknowledged the quality of the education they received.

The students studied under Thomas Eyre, John Daniel and John Lingard (1771–1851). Lingard is noted as a particularly brilliant scholar and historian. Hogarth later wrote:

> I learned more in one month than I had done in six under my former pedagogue; and I also remember that, while he [Lingard] was listening to me translating Latin into English, he was turning over the leaves of a large folio, and making notes for his history, and yet nothing escaped him of what I was reading.[5]

Lingard studied at Douai and travelled to the North-East after the French Revolution. He was ordained priest in York and taught at Crook Hall and thereafter at Ushaw, eventually as vice-president under Eyre. When Eyre died in 1810, Lingard became the acting president and expected to be confirmed in post, but the bishops thought he was too similar to his predecessor and appointed John Gillow as second president instead. On account of this, Lingard left Ushaw in 1811 for a parish in Hornby in Lancashire, where he spent the next forty years writing his famed *History of England* in eight volumes. Pope Pius VII promoted him to the rank of doctor three times: in theology, civil law and canon law![6]

Lingard is also noted for his disagreement with Cardinal Wiseman, the first Archbishop of Westminster, who Lingard believed was intent on "Romanizing" English Catholicism. Lingard objected to the introduction in England of a number of Roman practices (e.g. the wearing of the Roman clerical collar in public) and devotions: particularly the *Quarant' Ore*, the three-hours devotion on Good Friday, and Marian devotions throughout May. He also objected to the introduction of the Litany of Loretto, originating in the later Middle Ages and commonly in use in Rome, arguing that the devotional titles given to the Blessed Virgin Mary, such as "Mystical Rose", "Tower of David" and "House of Gold", were appellations that English Catholics would not understand. Wiseman in turn accused the Lingardians of "Gallicansim", a national Catholicism which failed to recognize the universality of the Church.

Hogarth received the tonsure and the four minor orders from Bishop William Gibson on 19 March 1807. The following year he was ordained sub-deacon (2 April 1808), shortly before moving, with the rest of the students and staff, to Ushaw, on 29 July 1808, to complete his training. Hogarth was appointed prefect of discipline and recalled that, on the first night at Ushaw, everyone had to go to bed in the dark for want of lamps. Bishop Gibson blessed the chapel, and the Revd Thomas Eyre was installed as the first president of the college.

In the winter of 1808–9, there was an outbreak of typhus which swept through northern England and arrived at the college early in the New Year. Five of the Ushaw students died within the space of a month, but Hogarth and his brother survived, although it is recorded that "Long vigils had to be kept by the bedside of several who came near to death, among them William Hogarth, the future Bishop of Hexham."[7] At Ushaw, Hogarth was ordained deacon on 14 December 1808, his brother Robert was ordained priest the following year (in March 1809), and William was ordained priest on 20 December 1809.

Before the restoration of the hierarchy in 1850, there were no dioceses and no parishes in Britain, and it was regarded by the Holy See as missionary territory. Hence the area centred on a Catholic chapel or church was known as "a mission". Originally it had been intended that Hogarth would serve the mission in Blackburn, but evidently he was highly regarded and was kept at Ushaw to join the staff, becoming prefect general. One of his pupils at the time was Nicholas Wiseman, later the first Cardinal Archbishop of Westminster. Staying on at a seminary for a couple of years after ordination was not altogether uncommon, and he would have been involved in the supervision of the younger pupils. He perhaps did some teaching too, as well as being involved in the liturgical life of the college.

In 1811, Hogarth was appointed procurator or bursar, which was no easy task when the new college had so little money. Later he recalled that with all his duties he was seldom in bed before twelve at night or after five the following morning. He also recalled trembling "whenever I heard the kitchen door opening lest it be a creditor coming for his remittance when all I had was a few shillings".[8] Nevertheless, during this time in his life Hogarth learnt about administration and financial frugality and prudence, skills that would serve him well in later life.

Hogarth finally left Ushaw, possibly on the brink of mental and physical collapse, in October 1816 to serve as chaplain to the Witham family at Cliffe Hall in the (Church of England) parish of Manfield. There was no Catholic church in the little Yorkshire village of Cliffe, but there was a Catholic chapel at Cliffe Hall. A nineteenth-century source recorded "Cliffe in the parish of Manfield wapentake of Gilling West, and liberty of Richmondshire; (the seat of Henry Witham Esq.) 1½ miles NNW of Manfield and 6 miles WNW of Darlington. Here is no place of worship except a catholic chapel, the Rev William Hogarth Minister. Cliffe Hall, Pop. 53."[9] The hall, which traces its origins to the thirteenth century, came into the possession of the Witham family in the fifteenth century. Henry Witham Esquire, born Henry Silvertop, was from a Catholic family, and spent much of his time in Edinburgh, where he was elected a Fellow of the Royal Society of Edinburgh (FRSE) for his amateur work in palaeontology and mineralogy. He married Eliza Witham, daughter of Thomas Witham and niece and heiress of William Witham, and hence Henry inherited the Witham name, the coat of arms and Cliffe Hall. In addition to serving the Witham family, Hogarth would have served other Catholics in the vicinity too.

In 1823, Hogarth was appointed to the mission at Darlington, with instructions that the Cliffe Hall mission and the Darlington mission should be amalgamated. In the first instance, Hogarth remained resident at Cliffe Hall, but in 1824 Cliffe Hall was sold, the Cliffe and Darlington missions were united and Hogarth moved to Darlington, as the first "incumbent of the united congregations of Cliffe and Darlington".[10] The Darlington mission was founded in 1783, and Mass was originally celebrated in the premises of a prominent Catholic family, the Ridsdales. On the Return of 1780, forty-three Catholics were recorded in Darlington.[11] Subsequently, and as the number of Catholics increased, there was a purpose-built chapel at "Bondgate" (probably dating from about 1809) behind 40 Coniscliffe Road, to which Hogarth moved. The local community was fast outgrowing this little chapel, but fortunately there was adjacent land available and, according to research undertaken by Mr G. Wild and resulting in *The Darlington Catholics*, it was on 17 June 1825 that a piece of land, formerly part of Green Tree Field (72ft by 45ft), was sold by Harry Vane, Earl of Darlington, and Henry Viscount Barnard to Thomas Penswick, John Yates and William Hogarth. The price was £55, and this was the first of a series of purchases to secure the whole of the corner plot, now at the corner of Coniscliffe Road and Larchfield Street.

Money was raised by the indefatigable Hogarth, and the building of a church designed by Ignatius Bonomi began in early 1826. Built of limestone with a Westmorland slate roof, the church was austere in a simplified, non-archaeological, pre-Puginian Gothic style. It was a combination of strength and elegance enhanced by an oak-panelled ceiling. The building work progressed rapidly and, in April 1827, Hogarth wrote to Bishop Smith to tell him the new chapel would be dedicated to St Augustine and asking him to open it. The bishop duly obliged, with great solemnity, on 29 May 1827. There was a congregation of citizens of the town and the Revd Richard Gillow, a professor from Ushaw and a "young gentleman of great attainment", preached the sermon. A collection was taken, which amounted to £31, and went towards the building fund. In October, the chapel was registered in the Durham Quarter Sessions as a place of worship, for Catholics, and the 1851 Ordnance Survey records a chapel with a capacity of 450 seats.[12] Today the Catholic churches in Darlington are part of the "Hogarth Partnership".

In 1830, Hogarth's bishop offered to move him to a wealthier parish in Hull, but having built his chapel, Hogarth chose to remain in Darlington ministering to, and building up, his fledgling Catholic community. As well as Irish immigrants, there was a steady flow of English converts to Catholicism, sometimes on account of marriage, at one point as many as twenty-five or thirty a year.

In 1842, Hogarth founded St Augustine's Primary School, which catered at that time for about 140 pupils. More land was subsequently bought, and the school was extended. As Hogarth considered education a significant part of his work, both in Darlington and later, it is worth considering a little more closely. There was, at that time, a large number of Irish immigrant workers in the North-East, and hence there was a significant number of Catholics and Catholic children too. Furthermore, these children were not well-to-do, but poor, and Hogarth recognized an obligation towards them.

First, he saw it as a matter of salvation. He wrote, "We shudder when we think of it, that every year thousands of Catholic children are trained up in error, or sunk in the depths of vice and immorality, because their parents or their pastors are unable to procure for them the blessing of a religious education."[13] Furthermore, he recognized the faithful had need of, and indeed a right to, the sacraments, and Catholic schools made this possible.

Second, Hogarth recognized a charitable dimension to education; that is to say he saw it as an essential part of Catholic social teaching: part of a pastoral programme which involved visiting the sick, supporting those in poverty and evangelizing the lapsed. As a priest and later as a bishop, he recognized education to be his particular responsibility as a pastor. Furthermore, he was not reticent to appeal to his congregations for funds, and he made the connection between self-denial and almsgiving, particularly in Lent. "Alms giving for the poor ... was for him both an act of charity and one of penance, a genuinely spiritual act to bring one into a closer communion with The Lord",[14] and Hogarth was active in raising funds for Catholic schools and education.

Later, as a newly appointed bishop, Hogarth would greet the announcement of government grants for Catholic schools in 1848 by issuing a pastoral letter to the Northern Vicariate in which he laid down the principles which I have outlined above: that it was not merely charitable to contribute to the education of the poor, but an intrinsic part of their pastoral and spiritual care; part of the social work of the Church:

> It is then, the duty of all Catholics, who value the great blessings of Education ... to make every effort to meet the benevolent intentions of Government, now, for the first time, offering to assist in the education of the Catholic poor. Natural compassion for our brethren urges us, a deep conviction of the necessity of Education loudly calls upon us, and Religion commands us to contribute liberally to the Christian Education of our poor.[15]

Additionally, we might also observe that Hogarth invited the Sisters of Mercy from Cork to set up religious houses and schools in his diocese. Houses were established in Sunderland, Hexham and Durham, and, by the end of Hogarth's episcopacy, in 1866, there were seven schools throughout the diocese. In many ways, this is a story in itself, but it underlines Hogarth's determination and ability to put his educational principles into practice at that time. And it also underlines the value that he attached to his own education at Ushaw.

Finally, Hogarth is noted for the establishment, along with the Quaker Joseph Pease, of a Mechanics' Institute. This shows that not only was Hogarth interested in the basic education of children, but that he was also concerned with the education of artisans and workmen, and the employment (indeed emancipation!) of Catholics in the expanding local industries, particularly the railway.

Hogarth's work was obviously well regarded, and he was extremely popular: a genuine pastor of his people. His way of life in Darlington included a period in the confessional every morning before daily Mass and between the two Masses on Sunday. His accommodation was small and sparsely furnished. Hogarth modelled himself on the noted pastor and Catholic educationalist St Francis de Sales, who was his "patron saint".

The Catholic population of Darlington expanded and grew—from 200 in 1824 to 3,000 in 1866. Records from canonical visitations give a breakdown of all the figures, carefully recorded by Hogarth, but all the numbers need not concern us here. Moreover, Hogarth was noted for his personal kindness, and he generously supported all good causes in Darlington.

In 1838, Hogarth was appointed Vicar General to Bishop John Briggs (1788–1861), who was Titular Bishop of Trachis and the Vicar Apostolic of the Northern District. Wild describes the situation: "From this point the simple missioner became the bishop's principal administrative assistant responsible for the day to day running of the District's affairs in the four northern counties."[16] "Simple" seems inappropriate to me as a description of Hogarth, but points to the sheer complexity of the Vicar General's task. Wild explains that there was really no appropriate structure of ecclesiastical government at the time, very little money, fierce independence amongst some of the missioners, a growing Catholic population on account of immigration, the roads were bad and the railway in its infancy. Added to this, Hogarth had to maintain his mission in Darlington on top of his role as Vicar General. But Hogarth was popular and tremendously hard-working and applied himself to the task.

In 1840, the number of districts or vicariates in England was doubled from four to eight by Pope Gregory XVI and the Northern District was split into three: Lancashire, Yorkshire and the "new" Northern. Briggs was translated to become Vicar Apostolic for the Yorkshire District. Subsequently, at the restoration of the hierarchy in 1850, he became the first Bishop of Beverley.

Rome appointed Henry Weedall, president of Oscott College, Birmingham, to succeed Briggs as Vicar Apostolic, but as Wild puts it, "had Beelzebub himself been appointed it could not have caused a greater fury".[17] Weedall, who did not want the appointment anyway, was seen as a puppet of Wiseman's intent on Romanizing the Church in England as discussed above. The northern clergy were having none of it and letters were duly dispatched. On some accounts, Rome eventually capitulated, on others Weedall declined the vicariate on grounds of ill-health. Either way, Bishop Francis Mostyn (1800–47), who was Titular Bishop of Abydus, was appointed as Vicar Apostolic in succession to Briggs, and Hogarth remained Vicar General.

But Mostyn himself was a timid and sickly man, and indeed on account of his health spent four or five months each year in the south of England or in France. This put an even greater strain on Hogarth, and necessary decisions could not be made when Mostyn was absent. Hogarth remarked in a letter to Bishop Briggs that "a state of headlessness existed in the District".[18] Despite his age, Hogarth's workload was prodigious and showed no signs of diminishing. He was, during this time, also actively involved with establishing a new Catholic community at Bishop Auckland.

Eventually, Mostyn died in office in Durham, on 11 August 1847, and was buried in Ushaw. He was succeeded by right by Bishop William Riddell (1807–47), who was Titular Bishop of Lagania and coadjutor Vicar Apostolic to Briggs. Tragically, he contracted cholera while ministering to the victims of an epidemic in Newcastle and died just under three months later, on 2 November 1847.

For a further eight months, the district was without a bishop, and Hogarth acted as administrator until the following year, when he was ordained as Titular Bishop of Samosata in the chapel at Ushaw on 24 August 1848 and appointed Vicar Apostolic. The principal consecrator was Bishop Briggs (at the time Vicar Apostolic for the Yorkshire District), assisted firstly by Bishop George Brown, at the time Titular Bishop of Tlos and Vicar Apostolic for the Lancashire District, and subsequently the first Bishop of Liverpool. Bishop William Wareing also assisted, being at the time Titular Bishop of Areopolis and Vicar Apostolic for the Eastern District, and subsequently the first Bishop of Northampton.

Despite his prowess as an administrator and his capacity for hard work, physically Hogarth appeared small, rather ordinary, and even untidy in his appearance. It is estimated that he was about 5' 6" to 5' 8" tall; he had broad shoulders, muscular arms, and big hands with prominent knuckles. His face is described as a paradox. A "strong jaw shows obstinacy, pugnacity and a will to command and be obeyed. His eyes, however, are gentle, probably grey, which in concert with his mouth could give the whole face a charming, almost avuncular look."[19]

Two years later, the Catholic hierarchy was restored, and Hogarth was translated (on 29 September) to be the first Bishop of Hexham. St Mary's Church, Newcastle, became the cathedral. It is worth noting that, by this time in his career, Hogarth knew his own mind. First, Rome favoured calling the new see Newcastle, but Hogarth preferred Hexham as "by far the most central and easy of access by means of railroad from all parts of the District".[20] For the time being, Hogarth's view prevailed. Second, it is perhaps significant that Hogarth moved to neither Hexham nor Newcastle, but remained resident at St Augustine's Presbytery in Darlington. He is noted for having been the first of the restored hierarchy to sign a public document "William, Bishop of Hexham" in defiance of the Ecclesiastical Titles Act (1851), which made it an offence for anyone outside the "United Church of England and Ireland" to use any episcopal title "of any city, town or place ... in the United Kingdom".

Bishop Hogarth sent his first pastoral letter to his diocese on 14 November 1850. It was principally concerned with a plan to raise money for the maintenance and upkeep of the churches and schools of the diocese. A final paragraph tells the people of his "unworthy" appointment and asks for their prayers. Hogarth's considerable workload continued, but by now he was able to make his own appointments and arrange assistance. Notably, Robert Tate, who would go on to be the sixth president of Ushaw, was appointed as bishop's secretary, and Robert Cornthwaite (later Bishop of Beverley) served as Vicar General.

In 1861, Hexham diocese was renamed the Diocese of Hexham and Newcastle, and Hogarth became the first bishop of the new diocese. The cathedral remained at St Mary's, Newcastle and was a centre for spiritual growth and devotion, as was nearby St Andrew's. A variety of religious associations was established: the Confraternity of the Blessed Sacrament, the Confraternity of Religious Doctrine, a rosary group, guilds of the Blessed Virgin Mary and of the scapular, and an SVP (St Vincent de Paul) group. These were not solely devotional groups but were also involved in ministry, particularly visiting the sick.

Hogarth is remembered as a hugely energetic and capable administrator. It is said that every church and chapel was either built or enlarged under his management. In 1851, there were seventy priests in the diocese, including the eleven at Ushaw, fifty-one public chapels and only three convents. By 1866, there had been a 30 per cent increase in the clerical body, to 102 priests, while the number of public chapels had gone up by 60 per cent to eighty-one, and there were eleven convents.[21] It has been estimated that Mass attendance doubled between 1851 and 1861.

Another significant event at this time was the restoration of a Dominican house in Newcastle. The Order of Preachers was founded by Dominic de Guzmán (1170–1221), and this is usually dated to 1216, when Dominic and his companions adopted the Rule of St Augustine (hence the cream Dominican habit—it's their black *cappa* that gives the name Black Friars). This was confirmed on 22 December 1216, when Pope Honorius III recognized the new order by his Bull *Religiosam Vitam*.

The first Dominican Friars arrived in England in 1221 and established houses in Oxford (1221), London (1223), Edinburgh (1230) and Cambridge (1238), and later in Newcastle (1239), Glasgow (1246) and Leicester (1247). These, of course, were all suppressed at the Protestant

Reformation. In the late nineteenth century, the Friars returned to the United Kingdom, re-establishing many of their medieval houses, firstly in London (1860) and then in Newcastle (1861). Bishop Hogarth invited the Friars to return to Newcastle, and at first they were based at, and ran, Old St Andrew's in Worswick Street, but in 1865 the Red Barns site, overlooking a part of Hadrian's Wall, was secured. A new church by Dunn and Hanson, costing £15,000 and dedicated to St Dominic, was built in the northern European transitional Romanesque-Gothic style. The foundation stone was laid in 1869, and the church was blessed and opened on 11 September 1873 by Archbishop (later Cardinal) Henry Manning. In 1882, the Dominican house was raised to the status of a priory.

Bishop Hogarth remained a very keen supporter of the work of the college at Ushaw, and although here is not the place to go into all the details, he defended it as a diocesan seminary, ultimately under his control as bishop, in opposition to those who saw Ushaw as a seminary for the North controlled by a board of bishops.[22] Hogarth supported his friend and former pupil Charles Newsham, who had become the fifth president at Ushaw. Hogarth encouraged Newsham to undertake considerable expansion and building works between 1848 and 1858. He advocated independence of the college and aimed to put it on a sound financial footing, insisting in particular that students from outside the diocese should be financially supported by their own bishop.

He was a little older than his episcopal colleagues and tended not to involve himself in the wider issues of the day, but concentrated on running his diocese, rather in the style of the old Vicars Apostolic. He "proved himself as an efficient administrator serving the diocese of Hexham and Newcastle with courage and zeal".[23] Perhaps it was this that caused one of his very few critics to give him the nickname "Pumpkin the Pompous".[24] In general, he was well respected by his episcopal colleagues and was a friend and confidant of his former pupil, Nicholas (later Cardinal Archbishop) Wiseman.

In 1863, Hogarth celebrated his seventy-seventh birthday, and Francis Mewburn wrote in his diary:

> This 25th is the birthday of my old and valued friend Right Rev. Bishop Hogarth and my near neighbour. I have known him full forty years and have been & continue on terms of the greatest intimacy with him. I do not remember or record a more truly gentlemanly man, and a better or trustier friend does not exist. When he reminded me of his birthday I replied 'Sincerely long, very long may you live and happy may you be.'[25]

Bishop Hogarth died without long illness, although he was just short of eighty years of age. He was seen walking around Darlington, conversing with people he knew on the Saturday. The following day he offered the parish Mass as usual. In the afternoon, he was struck "with an attack of paralysis", as he was writing to the president of Ushaw, Robert Tate: "Every letter was correctly formed until near the end, when the pen made a crooked stroke as he fell on the floor."[26] Although he rallied somewhat, he died peacefully the following day (29 January 1866) at a quarter to four in the afternoon.

His body lay in state in his own church of St Augustine in Darlington on 30 and 31 January, and a solemn Requiem Mass was celebrated on 1 February. The sermon was preached by Hogarth's chaplain, Fr Henry Coll, and was described as lengthy and full of emotion. Coll had to pause several times to overcome his emotions. The church was full, and tickets had been issued to avoid overcrowding. The sermon was published in *The Darlington & Stockton Times*.

After the requiem, Hogarth's body was transferred to Ushaw through the streets of Darlington, which were impassable so dense was the crowd, all wishing to pay a final tribute to their much-loved bishop. The Anglican church of St Cuthbert rang a muffled bell to mark the bishop's passing. The coffin left Darlington at 1 p.m. in a procession of some fifteen carriages and coaches and arrived at Ushaw at 7 p.m. On the following day, after another Mass and a sermon by Bishop Ullathorne (Bishop of Birmingham), Hogarth's body was interred in the cloisters of Ushaw College cemetery.

Robert Tate would later recall in a letter to Canon Thomas Slater:

> The wind was so high that the coffin was borne to the cemetery without a pall ... it was really pleasing to see how the boys came to kneel near the bier and pray for his soul at any time they could do so and some said they felt as if they were in the company of a good old friend ... The dear good bishop was the last of that genuine, kind, unpretending, familiar and yet commanding all respect and affection, fatherly old school of bishops ... His remains rest near those of Bishops Mostyn & Smith & Gibson each under a blue flat stone. When all is quiet one can stand there and say a De Profundis and think of days gone by forever.[27]

At the present time, Ushaw College having now been closed as a seminary, the cemetery is perhaps a little forlorn, and I expect that those who pause to say a *De Profundis* are few. Nevertheless, the grass is mowed, and the cemetery maintained; there is a sense of peaceful repose, and the ground is hallowed by the bodies of the bishops. Furthermore, while the seminary days may have gone forever, Ushaw Historic House, Chapels and Gardens are re-inventing themselves, and there is a general sense of purpose about the place.

A monument to Bishop Hogarth was erected in Darlington. It is an obelisk of polished granite, 30ft high, designed by Edward Pugin, which bears the inscription:

> To the Rt Rev William Hogarth D.D., First Bishop of Hexham and Newcastle, the Father of his clergy and the poor, who by a saintly life, great labours and charity unbounded, won love and veneration from all. This monument was erected by his flock and fellow townsmen of every creed and party. Born at Dodding Green, Westmoreland, Died at Darlington 29 January 1866. Buried at St Cuthbert's College, Ushaw, aged 80 years. RIP.

Notes

1. *Oxford Dictionary of National Biography.*
2. Quoted in David Milburn, *A History of Ushaw College* (Ushaw, 1964), p. 41.
3. Ibid., p. 58.
4. Sheridan Gilley, "The Legacy of William Hogarth, 1786–1866", *Recusant History*, 25:2 (2000), pp. 249–62, here at p. 249.
5. Ibid.
6. See Michael J. Walsh, *The Westminster Cardinals* (London: Burns & Oates, 2008), p. 12.
7. Milburn, *History of Ushaw College*, p. 111.
8. Cited in the Revd H. Coll's funeral oration, *The Weekly Register*, 10 February 1866.
9. Colin Hinson (2006, 2010) The Ancient Parish of Manfield, at <https://www.genuki.org.uk/big/eng/YKS/NRY/Manfield>, accessed 3 December 2021.
10. Leo Gooch, *From Jacobite to Radical: The Catholics of North East England, 1688–1850* (Durham University, Ph.D. thesis, 1989), p. 155.
11. See G. Wild, *The Darlington Catholics* (Darlington: Carmel Convent, 1993), p. 35.
12. See ibid., pp. 52–4.
13. Hexham and Newcastle Diocesan Archive, "Pastoral Letters 1849–1850": Pastoral Letter, 7 February 1849.
14. Sean B. Power, *The development of Roman Catholic education in the nineteenth century, with some reference to the diocese of Hexham and Newcastle* (Durham University, MA dissertation, 2003), p. 119.
15. Hexham and Newcastle Diocesan Archive, "Pastoral Letters 1823–1849": Pastoral Letter, 18 June 1848.
16. Wild, *Darlington Catholics*, p. 59.
17. Ibid., p. 62.
18. Letter from Hogarth to Bishop Briggs, 18 March 1841, Leeds Diocesan Archives.
19. Wild, *Darlington Catholics*, pp. 49–50.
20. Letter from Hogarth to Bishop Grant, 20 September 1848, quoted in Wild, *Darlington Catholics*, p. 73.
21. See Gilley, "Legacy of William Hogarth", p. 258.
22. See ibid. for more details.

23 Milburn, *History of Ushaw College*, p. 269.
24 See ibid., p. 197.
25 Diary of Francis Mewburn, 25 March 1863, quoted in Wild, *Darlington Catholics*, pp. 77–8.
26 Quoted in Gilley, "Legacy of William Hogarth", p. 260.
27 Letter from Tate to Slater, 16 February 1866, UCH 138diii, UCA, quoted in Wild, *Darlington Catholics*, pp. 78–9.

2

James Chadwick (1866–82)

Bishop Hogarth was succeeded by James Chadwick, whose father John was from an old Catholic family from Lancashire: he was "one of the family of Chadwicks of Barth in Lancashire who came from Haslingden or Haselden in the same county".[1] He emigrated to Drogheda in Ireland and was prosperous in business, owning a flax mill, several linen mills and a linen manufacturing business. John Chadwick was one of the major employers in the area, and he lived in a large country home in Mornington, just outside the town. He and his family supported the work of the local Catholic church, and indeed they funded the building of a new church in the town.

John married Frances Dromgoole, of an old and persecuted Catholic family from Dromgoolestown, County Louth. Their third son was James Chadwick, born on 24 April 1813.

In May 1825, when just twelve years old, Chadwick was sent to school at St Cuthbert's College in Ushaw. Originally, he was enrolled as a lay pupil, but changed onto the clerical track. He received tonsure and the four Minor Orders at Ushaw at the hands of Bishop Briggs on 18 December 1835. He was, perhaps rather unusually, ordained sub-deacon the following day and then, and again by Briggs, deacon the following May. He was ordained priest, for the Northern District, on 17 December 1837.

Following ordination, Chadwick remained at the college in Ushaw, having been appointed as general prefect of the house by the then president Dr Youens. He would have been engaged in supervising the younger students and perhaps doing some teaching. He was presumably also engaged in further (what we might now call "postgraduate") study. After three years, he was appointed a teacher of humanities and later professor of philosophy. In 1849, he became vice-president of the college and professor of dogmatic theology.

After just a few months, his health broke down, and he resigned his position at the college to join a small group of secular priests (including Frs Robert Rodolph Suffield and Edward Consitt) at their house in Wooler in north Northumberland, not far from the Scottish border. This house had been originally founded by Mrs Jane Silvertop in 1792 and dedicated to St Ninian, with a chapel on the top floor. Later, Bishop William Hogarth established it as the Diocesan Mission Centre, and Chadwick was engaged in missionary and retreat work in Hexham and Newcastle, in Lancashire and Yorkshire and throughout the area. He became famous as a preacher. He is particularly remembered for his ministry to women religious and was a noted spiritual director. He was described as "quiet, reasonable, self-possessed and gentlemanly".[2] In 1856, the house at Wooler was badly damaged by fire and Chadwick returned to Ushaw once more as professor of philosophy.

In 1859, Chadwick left Ushaw again to take up the post of chaplain to Lord Stourton. William Stourton, the eighteenth baron and a prominent Catholic peer, indeed one of the first Catholic peers to take his seat in the Lords after Catholic emancipation, died in 1846, passing the title to the nineteenth baron Charles Stourton (1802–72), who had married Mary Lucy Clifford in 1825. They had four children and lived at Allerton Castle in Allerton Park, near Knaresborough in Yorkshire, which was bought, in 1805, by the seventeenth Baron Stourton. Between 1843 and 1853, the castle was rebuilt by London architect George Martin in a Tudor Gothic style.

It would have been the case that Fr Chadwick would have ministered to the spiritual needs of Lord Stourton and his family and the Catholics who lived nearby. The work would not have been overly taxing, and Bishop Alexander Goss of Liverpool wrote to Chadwick, urging him to put his talents to better use, even offering him an appointment in Southport, but Chadwick declined.[3]

At this time, Chadwick was elected as a canon of the then diocese of Beverley. Established in 1850, with the episcopal see fixed at the pro-cathedral of St George in York, the first bishop was John Briggs. In 1861, he was succeeded by Robert Cornthwaite, who was bishop until 1878, when the see was dissolved, the territory being divided between the new dioceses of Leeds and Middlesbrough.

In 1863, Chadwick was invited to return to Ushaw, under the new president Robert Tate, for a little more teaching, this time as professor of pastoral theology, until, in 1866, he was appointed as the second Bishop of Hexham and Newcastle, *per obitum Hogarth*. Rome confirmed the appointment on 12 August 1866, and Chadwick was ordained bishop in the chapel at Ushaw on 28 October 1866, by Archbishop Manning, assisted by Bishops William Turner (Salford), Robert Cornthwaite (Beverley), Thomas Grant (Southwark), James Brown (Shrewsbury) and Francis Amherst (Northampton), who preached the sermon.

He was enthroned in St Mary's Cathedral, Newcastle on 8 November 1866 and took up residence at the Bishop's House at 72 Rye Hill. Chadwick had been a bishop for less than a year when, on 7 June 1867, he was honoured and named as Assistant to the Papal Throne, by Blessed Pope Pius IX. This was an ecclesiastical title for prelates belonging to the papal chapel and serving near the papal throne at solemn functions. The Assistants ranked immediately below the College of Cardinals and were also considered Counts at the Apostolic Palace, that is, they were considered as papal nobility. Pope Paul VI abolished these ranks in the reforms of the 1960s, but Chadwick's appointment so early in his episcopal career must reflect the high esteem in which he was held.

The following year, he was appointed a Council Father at the First Vatican Council. This was convoked by Blessed Pope Pius IX in 1869, but suspended indefinitely (although never formally closed) in 1870, when Italian troops occupied Rome and war broke out between France and Prussia. The Council was not convened to deal with any immediate or pressing crisis, but had intended to treat a wide variety of themes. Two in particular were prominent. Firstly, the linked issues of the nature of the Church and the nature of the papacy. These had perhaps not been treated as thoroughly as they might have been by the previous Council (of Trent 1545–63) and, in the light of the re-unification of Italy which had considerably reduced the Papal States to a small enclave, Pope Pius IX wanted to strengthen the papacy, and in doing so was significantly supported by Henry Manning, whom he had secretly consulted before the Council.[4] Strangely, Manning was not even a bishop when the Council was announced, and English bishops were not really consulted, but some months later, after his appointment, he became a staunch supporter of the cause. It is even said that, on the steps of St Peter's, after Vespers for St Peter and St Paul, Manning "made a vow to commit himself to achieving the declaration of papal infallibility".[5]

Secondly, in the light of the scientific revolution of the seventeenth century, the humanist Enlightenment of the eighteenth, and the havoc wrought by the French Revolution, the question of the relationship between faith and reason was ripe for consideration again.

In the end, the Council only produced two short decrees. "The Dogmatic Constitution on the Catholic Faith" sought to steer a middle way between the extremes of rationalism and fideism, emphasizing two sources of knowledge: natural and divine. This has always been a difficult dichotomy to bridge, and the Second Vatican Council would later emphasize the unity of knowledge and life, consonant with scripture and the teaching of the early fathers of the Church.[6] The "First Dogmatic Constitution on the Church of Christ", which did not, in fact, have any sequels as originally intended, dealt with the papacy in four sections. The first three are perhaps relatively uncontroversial, but in the fourth section the infallible teaching authority of the Roman Pontiff was defined, which was, and still is, highly controversial.

Here is not the place to discuss this controversy in detail, but suffice it to say that there were those (the "infallibilists") centred around Cardinal Manning, and including Chadwick, who were all in favour of the declaration: Manning believed that "all papal pronouncements, even if not infallible, required from Catholics interior consent".[7] Indeed Manning had become a Catholic seeking freedom from religious error! There were those who were firmly opposed to the doctrine, particularly the Bishop of Rottenburg in Germany, Karl Joseph von Hefele (1809–93), whose opposition was significant because he was an expert on the history of the Councils of the Church. Finally, there were those who, for whatever reasons, thought that a formal definition was not expedient (*"non expedit"*).

John Henry Newman in particular, although neither a bishop nor at the Council, and not in principle opposed to the teaching, was wary of pronouncing a definition. He objected to "a sweeping application of infallibility to all the pronouncements of any Pope and the way in which proponents of such views anathematized everyone else as unorthodox. Familiar as he was with the history of the early Councils [like von Hefele], Newman had no illusions that unity in the Church meant utter uniformity of ideas."[8] In a letter to W. G. Ward, Newman recommended the old maxim: *"in necessariis unitas, in dubiis libertas, in omnibus caritas"* (in necessary things unity, in doubtful things [e.g. infallibility!] liberty, in all things charity).

In the end, the definition was passed in Rome, but in a modified version, and many of those who opposed the definition stayed away from the final vote. Newman observed that "hitherto he has done what he would, because its limits were not defined—now he must act to rule", and we may also observe that this whole affair put further strain on Newman's already troubled relationship with Cardinal Manning, who "came back from Rome triumphant",[9] broadcasting the new doctrine in a very lengthy pastoral letter. Although Newman had written a letter opposing the doctrine before its declaration, he remained largely silent thereafter. Later, Henry O'Callaghan (see below) told Manning "that the notion of Newman's opposition to the Pope was now completely dispelled".[10]

On his return from the Council, Chadwick threw himself into the building up of his diocese. He began by conducting an exacting review of the diocese. There are forty-six surviving returns from Chadwick's visitation of 1868-9. The priests were each sent an "enquiry booklet" of formidable proportions with questions concerning their personal circumstances, parish property, finance and discipline; a request for an inventory of the church presbytery and school; and questions concerning finance and accounts. Although routine nowadays, this would have been a new departure in 1868!

The information gleaned from Bishop Chadwick's survey would have informed him and enabled the development of the diocese. During the sixteen years of his episcopate, the number of churches throughout Cumberland, Durham, Northumberland and Westmorland increased from 81 to 109. The number of clergy, secular and religious, increased from 96 to 158, and Chadwick consistently taught the sanctity of the priesthood and the importance of pastoral care. Communities of nuns, engaged in teaching and the care of the poor, increased from 11 to 26. Chadwick had a particular concern for orphaned and homeless children, and after his death the Bishop Chadwick School was founded to meet their particular needs.[11]

Bishop Chadwick also made a significant contribution to Catholic secondary education in Newcastle. Originally there had been no provision, but in order to accommodate boys who were too old to attend primary schools and who "refused to attend the Protestant schools",[12] a small Catholic school was opened in 1870. This was originally in Blackett Street opposite Eldon Square and Mr Lafferty, from the Liverpool Institute, was the first master. He died the following year and was succeeded by Mr J. M. Kelly, who moved the school to Westmorland Road in 1871. Eventually Kelly emigrated to America and the school closed, but the diocese bought the site and Bishop Chadwick formally opened St Cuthbert's Grammar School on 16 August 1881 at 62 and 64 Westmorland Road.

The first headmaster was Fr Wickwar, assisted by Fr Magill, and the school was very much a "child of Ushaw". Indeed the twofold purpose of the school was to be a feeder school to the northern seminary and to "enable our middle-class Catholic parents to educate their sons without detriment to their religion"![13] The liturgical observances at St Cuthbert's Grammar School were closely modelled on those at Ushaw, and there was the daily round of morning and evening prayer, visits to the Blessed Sacrament, the Litany of Our Lady on Saturday etc. It would also seem that Chadwick did not just found this school and let the masters get on with it; he was a regular visitor, frequently celebrating Mass and assisting practically as and when difficulties arose. Bishop Chadwick's love for the school was not confined to words, "but by every means in his power did he make it his endeavour to further the interests of the school".[14]

Chadwick is also noted for having written a handful of publications, which Brady describes as "some small but very useful works on Catholic doctrine".[15] In 1871, Chadwick edited Celestine Leuthner's *Coelum Christianum* (1759). Leuthner was a German Benedictine monk whose text is an extended meditation on the life, passion and death (*Vita, doctrina passio D. N. Jesu Christi*) of Jesus considered through the lens of the liturgical calendar.

In 1878, he published a slim volume, *St Teresa's Own Words: Or Instruction on the Prayer of Recollection*. Teresa of Avila was a Carmelite nun born in 1515. When asked to write about prayer, she professed to have "neither the health nor the intelligence for it",[16] but she wrote under obedience, and *The Interior Castle* is a recognized spiritual classic. Chadwick's text on St Teresa is based on the twenty-eighth and twenty-ninth chapters of St Teresa's *Way of Perfection* (1577), which in her own words describe methods for achieving prayer of recollection and set down some of the means by which we can make it a habit. To St Teresa's text, Chadwick added some very brief notes of his own, which clearly link the practice of interior prayer to living the virtuous life and perhaps give something of an insight into Chadwick's own spirituality. Additionally, *Instructions on how to Meditate* was published anonymously. These two volumes would have been aimed, first and foremost, at students for the priesthood at Ushaw and elsewhere.

Finally, Chadwick wrote a small number of hymns and carols, of which "Angels we have heard on High" is perhaps the best known. It is a loose translation of a traditional French carol of unknown origin (*Les Anges dans nos campagnes*), which tells of the birth of Jesus according to the Lucan tradition and is usually sung to the tune "Gloria", a French tune arranged by Edward Shippen Barnes.

In 1877, Chadwick returned to Ushaw for a year as president. The sixth president, Robert Tate, had died of cancer in 1876, and the Northern Bishops appointed Fr Francis Wilkinson to succeed him. Wilkinson had worked for many years in Ushaw's junior house and was reluctant to take on the role of president, although he was popular amongst staff and seminarians. It is said that "after learning of the bishops' decision he returned to his room broken hearted and weeping like a child".[17] Anyway he took on the role and attempted to remedy the poor state of the college chapel, but the following year he succumbed to typhoid fever and died on 23 September 1877.

"The two superiors of the house having died within such a short space of time of each other, the bishops had unusual difficulty in finding a successor."[18] They appointed a Canon Birkdale, a priest of the Liverpool diocese, but he refused the appointment. In view of this crisis, the governors, the Northern Bishops, asked Chadwick, on account of his long association with the college, to be the eighth president. He accepted but found the workload of college president, alongside that of bishop, too much. Unable to give his full attention to the college, he resigned the following year. His portrait at Ushaw shows him as silver-haired and sagacious in appearance, resplendent in *cappa magna*.

There is something of a question mark over Chadwick's health, which has been described as delicate. As we have seen, he withdrew from Ushaw in 1849, having been appointed vice-president, with poor health. A further health scare prompted his reception of the last rites shortly after his ordination as bishop and, towards the end of his life, he suffered from deteriorating health. After a severe attack of bronchitis, Bishop Chadwick died on 14 May 1882 in the bishop's residence at 72 Rye Hill, Newcastle upon Tyne. His body was "laid out in all its pontifical regalia, looking calm and beautiful as his sainted predecessor Cuthbert must have looked when years after his death, the monks were privileged to gaze on the incorrupt countenance of their father in Christ".[19]

Fr Edward Consitt, the cathedral provost and Chadwick's lifelong friend and colleague, preached the sermon at the funeral on the text "*Memento Domine, David et omnis mansuetudinis ejus*" ("Remember O Lord in David's favour, his humility", Ps. 131 (132):1). Consitt described Bishop Chadwick as a saintly man: mild-mannered and of great humility and yet nevertheless "every inch a bishop". He had a gift for friendship which extended to his colleagues, the students at Ushaw and to all who sought his counsel or advice. Chadwick avoided religious and political argument, and is not remembered for any spectacular achievements, but was faithful to the daily discharge of his duties as bishop. Consitt likened his life to the "unruffled course of a beautiful inland river . . . shedding light and gladness on every side, and making beautiful the landscape".

He was sixty-nine years old and had been Bishop of Hexham and Newcastle for almost sixteen years. From probate records, his wealth at his death was £587 16s 1d. Following his Requiem Mass and funeral, on the Tuesday after his death, he was solemnly borne through the streets of Newcastle, and the bells of St Nicholas' Anglican church tolled as the funeral cortège passed by. At his own choice, he was buried at Ushaw, in the shadow of the cemetery cross, a spot which he had long since chosen.

The cemetery at Ushaw had been established when the college was first built, and the first burials took place during the typhus epidemic of 1809. In 1852, the cloister was added, and in 1885 funds were provided for the extension of the cemetery and the memorial plaques in the cloister. The memorial cross, designed by Canon Scruton, was installed around 1870. Bishop Chadwick's tomb, erected in 1884, is notable. It was designed by the architect Archibald Dunn, based on the tomb of Godfrey de Bouillon in the Holy Sepulchre at Jerusalem. Chadwick and Dunn had visited the Church of the Holy Sepulchre together, and Chadwick had said this was the kind of tomb he would like for himself!

There were many who thought that Consitt would succeed his esteemed friend. Rome, however, decided otherwise, and Pope Leo XIII selected Dr John William Bewick VG to be the third Bishop of Hexham and Newcastle.

Notes

1. W. M. Brady, *Annals of the Catholic Hierarchy in England and Scotland AD 1585–1876* (London: John Mozley Stark, 1883), p. 414.
2. David Milburn, *A History of Ushaw College* (Ushaw, 1964), p. 285.
3. See *The Correspondence of Alexander Goss, Bishop of Liverpool, 1856–1872*, ed. Peter Doyle, p. 242.
4. See Meriol Trevor, *Newman's Journey* (Glasgow: Collins, 1974), p. 232.
5. Michael J. Walsh, *The Westminster Cardinals* (London: Burns & Oates, 2008), p. 55.
6. See Norman Tanner, *New Short History of the Catholic Church* (London: Burns & Oates, 2011), p. 221.
7. Walsh, *Westminster Cardinals*, p. 54.
8. Trevor, *Newman's Journey*, p. 235.
9. Ibid., p. 242.
10. Ibid., p. 247.
11. See Chadwick's entry in *The Oxford Dictionary of National Biography*.
12. Charles Hart, *The Early Story of St Cuthbert's Grammar School* (London: Burns & Oates, 1941), p. 2.
13. Ibid., p. 5.
14. Ibid., p. 6.
15. Brady, *Annals of the Catholic Hierarchy*, p. 415.
16. *Butler's Lives of the Saints: New Full Edition* (London: Burns & Oates, 1997), p. 99.
17. Milburn, *A History of Ushaw College*, p. 284.
18. Ibid., p. 285.
19. Hart, *Early Story of St Cuthbert's Grammar School*, p. 12.

3

John William Bewick (1882–6)

Bishop Chadwick was succeeded by John William Bewick, who was born on 20 April 1824 at Ministeracres, near Consett, in Northumberland. The Bewick family was a large and extended family, which has been the subject of much research. Bewick's father, also John William Bewick (1786–1855), was gamekeeper and steward at the Ministeracres estate, an eighteenth-century mansion built by George Silvertop. One of Bishop Bewick's brothers, Thomas John (1821–96), was a noted civil and mining engineer.

Ministeracres was and is an eighteenth-century mansion house. Originally built in 1758 by George Silvertop as a two-storey building, a third storey was added in 1811, and a new north wing was built in 1865. The Silvertops were a notable Catholic family; George was the first Catholic to be appointed High Sherriff of Northumberland, and it is more than likely that young John Bewick would have had a Catholic upbringing. The house was sold by the Silvertop family in 1949 and became a Passionist monastery, and later links were established with the Sisters of Mercy in Sunderland. Since 2012, the house has been a prayer and retreat centre.

The future Bishop Bewick studied at Ushaw and was ordained priest there on 27 May 1850, for the Northern District just months before the diocese of Hexham was restored. Bewick remained at Ushaw as a tutor for three years and was regarded as a brilliant Latin scholar, able to expound, defend and object in fluent Latin. He was characteristically very modest about this, and indeed he was known among his contemporaries as "silent John".[1] For years after he left Ushaw, he maintained contact with the college, serving as an external examiner.

In 1853, he was appointed assistant priest at the cathedral. Newcastle at the time was characterized by poverty, a lack of sanitation and overcrowded housing. There was an outbreak of cholera that killed hundreds. Bewick himself caught the disease but survived the ordeal, although it took some time for his health to be fully restored.

In 1855, Bewick was appointed rector of St Cuthbert's, North Shields. In the very early nineteenth century, Catholics in Tynemouth would have had to travel to Newcastle to go to Mass. However, the energetic Fr Worswick, who built the old St Andrew's Church in Newcastle (1796), now home to the university chaplaincy, set about establishing a more local provision for them and the foundation stone for St Cuthbert's, North Shields was laid in 1817. It was the first purpose-built Catholic church in the diocese outside Newcastle since the Reformation. The original building was demolished in the 1970s, and a modern church replaced it. The parish celebrated its bicentenary in 2017.

Bewick was appointed a canon of the diocese in 1865 and Vicar General in 1868. In 1869, Bishop Chadwick established a new parish dedicated to Our Lady and St Oswin in Tynemouth, and Bewick was sent there as the first parish priest in 1870. An ancient foundation dedicated to Our Lady and St Oswin at Jarrow, which housed the relics of St Oswin, a Christian king of Northumberland martyred in 651, was a significant centre of pilgrimage until it was closed at the Reformation. The dedication of this new parish recalled those earlier days. Originally, the new parish was based at a house on Front Street with a chapel to the rear. A new (albeit temporary) tin church was opened by Bishop Chadwick on 15 August 1871.

Bewick had always intended for a more permanent church to be built and indeed had acquired land for the purpose, but events overtook him, and he was unable to build the new church. That task was left to his successor, Canon George Howe, who built the permanent new church shortly after Bewick's death. The foundation stone was laid on 8 September 1889, and the new church of red brick in the simple lancet Gothic style, designed by E. J. Hansom, was opened and blessed by Bishop Wilkinson on 1 June 1890. The church cost £2,500, and since Howe was an able and keen musician, it contained a fine organ, built to Canon Howe's own specifications. Incidentally, Howe must have had something of a gift for building new churches, for he subsequently went on to establish the new parish (and church) of St Edward's in Whitley Bay. By 1898, Howe had bought some land in Whitley Bay and in 1899 received a legacy of £3,000 from Jane Collen which he used to build the church, which was eventually opened in 1911.

In addition to his parochial duties, this move to Tynemouth allowed Bewick to be nearer Bishop Chadwick, whom he served as secretary and most probably as diocesan treasurer (oeconomus) too. It was Bewick who established routine procedures and practices for the administration of the diocese. Bewick also drew up a map, dated 1876, showing for the first time the boundary of the diocese and the boundaries of each mission or parish. In some papers, Bewick also signs himself as diocesan archivist. It is clear that at this time he would have got to know the workings and the organization of the diocese very well, and indeed in the face of Chadwick's deteriorating health would have had to assume considerable responsibility. In 1875, the degree of Doctor of Divinity was conferred upon him by the Holy See.

It was therefore no great surprise that, following Chadwick's death, Bewick was appointed Bishop of Hexham and Newcastle in September 1882. His appointment had the unambiguous support of the diocesan chapter and the wider English episcopate, and his episcopal ordination took place on 18 October 1882. He was ordained by Cardinal Archbishop Manning assisted by Archbishop Charles Eyre (Glasgow) and Bishop Robert Cornthwaite (Leeds). This all took place in the cathedral and was an occasion of great solemnity:

> The Rev Robert Laing, Ushaw's dignified M.C. . . . saw to it that smoothness, dignity and precision marked every movement. Three of us from the Grammar School were chosen to act respectively as book-bearer, candle-bearer and crozier-bearer to the Cardinal, and, naturally enough prided ourselves on so distinguished an honour.[2]

Bishop Bewick maintained his residence at the presbytery in Front Street, Tynemouth, and from there he visited much, if not all, of his diocese. He wrote:

> The total population is no more than a million and a half. Of these 180,000 are of our fold and hear our voice and own allegiance in things spiritual. The diocese comprises an agricultural, a sea-faring, a manufacturing, a mining, an iron-working and a labouring population. The rich and opulent are few. If there are not large cities there are some of the busiest hives of industry in the world. Few rivers can vie in importance with the Tyne. There are 156 priests, 90 schools affording 27,500 scholars, but every day reveals the necessity of enlargement or multiplication. Ushaw College is our joy and our crown.[3]

Concerning the Grammar School, Bishop Bewick followed in the footsteps of his predecessor (indeed he was chairman of the Bishop Chadwick memorial fund committee) and "from the very outset he extended towards it [the school] his warmest support and ever took a lively interest in its welfare".[4] The bishop was instrumental in the move of January 1883, when the school, which had grown from fewer than fifty pupils to almost a hundred, moved from Westmorland Road to its new and present site in Bath Lane (formerly part of the Tyne Brewery Company) and the bishop had two rooms set aside for his use when he was required to be in Newcastle. His coat of arms was set above the entrance door, and it would seem he regarded himself as co-founder of the school with his predecessor.

Despite his brief term of office as bishop, Bewick established a number of new parishes at Blackworth, Haltwhistle, Tyne Dock, Witton Park and Windermere. The parish at Haltwhistle in Northumberland was established in 1860, and Fr Francis Kirsopp was appointed as the first parish priest, also serving Haydon Bridge. In the first instance, rented property was used for a Mass centre and school, but in 1884 a church dedicated to the Holy Cross was built. In 1902, a presbytery was completed, and the parish became known as St Wilfrid's, to distinguish it from the nearby Anglican church also dedicated to the Holy Cross.

In response to considerable industrial expansion in the area, St Peter and St Paul's parish, Tyne Dock, was established in 1885, and Mass was originally celebrated in the basement of the Exchange Building. A parish school with a chapel (designed by Charles Walker) and a presbytery were opened in 1889. The present church was opened in 1906 and consecrated by Bishop Thorman in 1930. Sacred Heart Church at Boldon Colliery was also served from Tyne Dock between 1896 and 1936.

The parish of St Chad at Witton Park was established in 1862 and eventually became part of the larger parish of St Mary and St Wilfrid, Bishop Auckland, until it closed in 1988. The parish of Our Lady and St Herbert at Windermere was part of the diocese of Hexham and Newcastle at its foundation in 1883, but became part of the diocese of Lancaster in 1924. The original church was replaced by a modern building in 1964.

In 1884, Bishop Bewick bought a big open field, on the Wolsingham Road, near the school, to be used as a Catholic cemetery known as Ashburton Cemetery. This was the first Catholic cemetery in the area and is now the place of rest of a number of Catholic clergy, as well as Catholic military personnel who fell in the two world wars. Bishop Bewick suffered from diabetes, long before the discovery of insulin, and his health declined steadily. He died suddenly, after only four years in office, in Bishop's House, Tynemouth on Friday 29 October 1886, with Canon Franklin from the cathedral at his bedside.

The Durham Directory of 1887 carried a record of Bewick's funeral, which took place on 2 November 1886. Bishop Lacy, the Bishop of Middlesbrough, celebrated a solemn sung Mass and Provost Consitt preached on Titus 1:7–8, outlining the qualities of a bishop. Following the Mass, and the five absolutions having been given, the body was borne to the hearse and transported, as was fitting, to the cemetery which he himself had established. The funeral cortège was estimated to have been almost a mile in length. It was met at the cemetery by Fr Wickwar and Fr Laing, who censed the coffin and sprinkled it with holy water before burial.

Following Bewick's death, the chapter appointed Provost Edward Consitt, mentioned above and a former Ushaw professor as Vicar Capitular, and he was again recommended to Rome as Bishop of Hexham and Newcastle. Again, this recommendation seemed to fall on deaf ears as the announcement was made that the rector of the Venerable English College, Dr Henry O'Callaghan, a complete stranger to North-East England, would be the fourth Bishop of Hexham and Newcastle.

Notes

1. See Brian Plumb, *Arundel to Zabi: A Biographical Dictionary of the Catholic Bishops of England and Wales (Deceased) 1623–2000* (Wigan: North West Catholic History Society, 1987, 2006), p. 33.
2. C. Hart, *The Early Story of St Cuthbert's Grammar School* (London: Burns & Oates, 1941), p. 15.
3. Plumb, *Arundel to Zabi*, p. 43.
4. Hart, *The Early Story of St Cuthbert's Grammar School*, p. 15.

4

Henry O'Callaghan (1887–9)

Henry O'Callaghan was perhaps the most unusual of all the bishops of Hexham and Newcastle, partly because of the shortness of his term of office and because he didn't ever take up permanent residence in the diocese! He was born in London of Irish parents on 29 March 1827, and "in spite of the O' in his name ... [he] ... prided himself on being an Englishman to the backbone."[1] He went to study at Old Hall Green, Ware, where he was ordained priest, for the Westminster archdiocese, on 15 March 1851. After ordination, he remained at the college as a "prefect", assisting with the younger students and perhaps teaching, which was not uncommon at that time.

St Edmund's, Ware found it origins, as explained above, at Douai College in France. Exiled from there, some of the staff went north to found a new college and some joined the Old Hall Green Academy at Ware. A gift of £10,000 from John Stone, a Hampshire Catholic, allowed new buildings (designed by James Taylor) to be constructed and a chapel by Pugin was designed and completed in 1853.

In 1852, a new vice-rector arrived at St Edmund's, and this would start a chain of events that would influence much of O'Callaghan's subsequent life. The new vice-rector was Herbert Vaughan. Previously, Vaughan had been studying for the priesthood in Rome, but he became ill and left Rome to return to England. Following petition to the Vatican, permission was obtained for Vaughan to be ordained priest at the very early age of twenty-two. On his return to England, Wiseman, the first Archbishop of Westminster following the restoration of the hierarchy in 1850, appointed Vaughan as vice-rector of St Edmund's, Ware.

Significantly, while he was in Rome, Vaughan had got to know Henry (later Cardinal) Manning, who had been Archdeacon of Chichester and was instrumental in the establishment of Chichester (Anglican) Theological College. He was received into the Catholic Church in 1851 and ordained priest later the same year. Five years later, the stories of Manning, Vaughan and O'Callaghan would converge. Wiseman knew of the Oblates of St Ambrose, which was an institute of secular priests founded by St Charles Borromeo (1538–84 and nephew of Pope Pius IV) whose members lived and worked together in Milan. This model had been imitated elsewhere, notably by the Oblates of St Hilary in Poitiers, France, and Wiseman was keen to establish a group of similar oblates, a band of missioners, in London, and he entrusted the task to Manning.

Manning established the London-based Oblates of St Charles at the end of 1856. The rule was practically the same as the original rule drawn up by St Charles himself, although adapted to English conditions, and it was approved by the Holy See in 1857 and confirmed, by Pope Pius IX, in 1877. The Oblates of St Charles were dissolved in the 1970s. Records from the very first chapter meeting of the Oblates (June 1857) exist, and alongside Manning were Herbert Vaughan, William W. Roberts, William Burke and Thomas McDonnell; and there were two students, two novices and two postulants. Manning was the superior of the Oblates and Vaughan the "quasi novice master".[2] Importantly for our story, the two novices were Thomas Dillon, who would succeed Manning as superior, and O'Callaghan, also recorded as an oblate novice.

Cardinal Wiseman installed the new group of Oblates (with Manning as their superior) at the church of St Mary of the Angels in Bayswater and they quickly threw themselves into the pastoral care of the people in the surrounding area, including the labourers who, at that time, were building Paddington station. Membership of Manning's group grew, and he and his oblates "completed his parish Church, and built three more churches. He established eight schools plus a choir school, opened four convents and set up a reformatory for Catholic boys."[3]

However, with Vaughan and O'Callaghan at Ware, the Oblates also became closely involved in the running of the St Edmund's seminary. O'Callaghan was prefect of discipline, and Vaughan was vice-president of the college. This might have been a good thing, but as it happened it did not turn out well. Ware was considered to be a 'diocesan seminary', although it was technically not a seminary (as defined three centuries earlier by the Council of Trent) as it had lay students, ordinary schoolboys, studying alongside the seminarians.[4] Nevertheless, there were those in the diocese who were concerned about the influence of the Oblates on a diocesan seminary: there was a concern that the Oblates might "recruit" the diocesan students. (It is surely no coincidence that one of the altars in the chapel was dedicated to St Charles Borromeo!) Apart from the question of undue influence, there were also disagreements about money. In the end, the Oblates withdrew from the seminary in 1861.

Vaughan embarked on a series of travels to raise money which he subsequently used to establish MHM, the Mill Hill Missionaries. For the record, Wiseman died in 1865, Manning was chosen as the second Archbishop of Westminster, and O'Callaghan was sent to Rome to be head of an Oblate house there. Very little is known about this short episode in O'Callaghan's life, except that at first the Oblates were based at S. Chiara and then at S. Nicola in Arcione, a church which no longer exists, but was not far from the Trevi Fountain. O'Callaghan returned to prominence when he was appointed rector of the Venerable English College (VEC) in 1867.

> The Venerable English College (the Venerabile) was founded in 1579, by Pope Gregory XIII, as a place to train priests for the English Mission, in a building which had formerly been a hospice to accommodate English pilgrims in Rome. It was, in a sense, an overflow institution for the English College in Douai. At the time of the Reformation, it was a criminal offence to return from Europe to England as a priest, and the early life of the college was sanctified by the blood of forty-four alumni who were martyred. The first of these was St Ralph Sherwin, who was martyred in 1581 alongside St Edmund Campion.

Following the restoration of the Catholic hierarchy in England in 1850, the VEC became "more distinguished for the production of bishops than of martyrs".[5] Cardinal Wiseman had been rector of the college. There was an old joke told to new students on their arrival at the college "about the three conditions necessary for being made a bishop: one, he must be a baptized Catholic (or ordained in alternate versions of the same story), two, he must be male, and three, he must be an alumnus of the *Venerabile*. The first two conditions could sometimes be dispensed with, the third never!"[6]

When O'Callaghan arrived at the *Venerabile* in 1867, he succeeded Fr Frederick Neve as rector. Neve had been Wiseman's appointment (in 1863) and, without going into all the particulars which are not relevant here, it seems Neve, although he had inherited a number of problems, made a success of his first few years as rector, and indeed student numbers almost doubled from twenty-four to forty-four.[7] However, in 1865 Wiseman died and the support Neve had received from Wiseman rather died too. Manning, who succeeded Wiseman, had rather different ideas about how seminarians should be trained and he considered that, under Neve, discipline at the college was poor, liturgical practice was lax and the students' general behaviour was not entirely becoming for seminarians.

The details are contested and, to a certain extent, Neve was probably just reflecting the attitudes of the prevailing culture under Wiseman. As time went on, however, Neve no longer had the support of his students, nor Manning and, perhaps more importantly, he lacked the support of the College Pro-Protector, Mgr George Talbot, a powerful English cleric in Rome who had the ear of Pope Pius IX. Eventually, under some pressure, Neve resigned in 1867.

Manning exerted his influence on Talbot, who advised the Pope, and O'Callaghan was appointed rector. Having said that, Talbot probably did not need much convincing: O'Callaghan's experience at Ware, his experience as an Oblate of St Charles, his knowledge of Rome and his ability to speak Italian were more than recommendations enough. It would appear that other bishops in Rome at the time were not consulted! Neve's vice-rector, Dr Giles, remained in post, and it seems that O'Callaghan and Giles were a perfect match as they reformed and improved the college. The *horarium* (timetable) was reformed; the food improved; restrictions on leaving the college for social excursion were put in place; and tighter financial controls were implemented. Canon Pocock observed O'Callaghan "was of distinguished appearance and carried himself with an air of superiority. His manner appeared haughty but this was only exteriorly. He was not the sociable type and did not care to make friends."[8] By contrast the vice-rector Dr Giles, now with an efficient, stern and fairly strict rector above him, was able to cultivate kindly relations with the students, and the situation improved all round.

Having said that, the new rector allowed celebrations at Christmas and "could thaw out on rare occasions and talk as affably as the next man; he might even provide the students with hot wine on a festive occasion; he was very kind-hearted when the occasion demanded some special attention on account of a student's health."[9] Although the student numbers remained small, the quality of the students improved and out of 105 students at the college between 1867 and 1887 no fewer than seven went on to become bishops, "and many held important posts in seminaries in England and abroad, as well as positions of responsibility in their dioceses".[10]

O'Callaghan had a number of other matters to deal with during his time as rector and it seems he coped with them all very well. As a man of his time, it seems he was a prolific letter-writer, but these were almost all letters pertaining to the financial business of the college. There was a time of war with the shelling and occupation of Rome itself, the rector of the Belgian College was stoned outside the *Collegio Romano*, and the university was turned out of its buildings and had to relocate. On a more peaceful note, Pope Pius IX visited the college to attend Bishop Grant on his deathbed and Cardinal (now St) John Henry Newman visited after receiving his cardinal's hat.

In 1881, there was a gathering of a large number of bishops at the college for the promulgation of the papal Bull *Romanos Pontifices*, which settled some sore points concerning the rights of the English bishops and religious congregations. In particular, Bishop Hubert Vaughan of Salford diocese, and later Cardinal Archbishop of Westminster, was opposed to the Jesuits opening a school in his diocese. However, the Jesuits were an "exempt" order, meaning they were answerable directly to the Pope. When the Jesuits went ahead and opened a school in Manchester in Vaughan's absence, he was furious. The English bishops appealed to Rome and, in a significant ruling, the Pope decreed that "when members of religious orders were working in a parish, they would be subject to the jurisdiction of the bishop".[11] Moreover, religious congregations who wished to open schools required the express permission of the local bishop.

In Rome, O'Callaghan acted as (joint) postulator of the cause of the beatification of some members of the college who had been martyred and the decree was signed in 1886. Lastly, O'Callaghan oversaw the rebuilding of the college chapel, which was completed in 1888. The first ceremony that took place in the new chapel was O'Callaghan's own ordination as bishop on 18 January 1888, by Cardinal Lucido Maria Parocchi, assisted by Bishop William Clifford, the third Bishop of Clifton, and Bishop John Vertue, the first Bishop of Portsmouth.

No doubt on account of the good job he had done at the college, O'Callaghan was appointed the fourth Bishop of Hexham and Newcastle following the death of Bishop Bewick. By all accounts, O'Callaghan did not want the job, and he was so anxious that he became unwell and the episcopal ordination, originally planned for 18 December 1887, had to be postponed. It seems that O'Callaghan tried to get out of his preferment altogether, but to no avail; he had to be obedient to his superiors, and he was finally ordained bishop. One eyewitness recalled:

> when it was nearly over, a lady who was near to me, and to whom I had just explained a few details of the function, suddenly said impetuously, 'How I hate it all'. For the moment I thought she was a Protestant, and simply said 'why?' The whispered answer came back 'Why can't they leave him here? You don't know what a friend he has been and how many will miss him.'[12]

On 17 February, O'Callaghan left Rome and travelled to his new diocese. He was enthroned in his cathedral on 18 March in what was described as "an inspiring ceremony, and one made still more awe-inspiring from the public avowal of the loyalty and fidelity of the clergy to one who had been placed over them by the Holy Father himself, and whose name had not even been on the *terna*".[13] Nevertheless, however inspiring it was to those who looked on, as the preacher compared the northerly climate in Newcastle with the blue skies of Rome, tears streamed down the new bishop's face. For O'Callaghan seminary life had been no preparation for running a diocese (remember he had not even ever run a parish!), and O'Callaghan appointed Canon Wilkinson as his Vicar General and would do nothing without his advice. Some ten weeks later, he returned to Rome and arranged for Wilkinson to be ordained as bishop and appointed as his auxiliary. Wilkinson was ordained on 25 July 1888. O'Callaghan returned to England for a time, but just one year later he resigned as Bishop of Hexham and Newcastle, on 27 September 1889. The role of bishop was beyond him.

Fr Hart poignantly recalls that, at the time, a nicely worded and neatly framed testimonial to Dr O'Callaghan was prepared by the masters and students of St Cuthbert's Grammar School for their new bishop. It was to be presented to him on the occasion of his first visit, which was daily expected with a flutter of joy. Alas, the bishop did not ever visit the school, and the unpresented testimonial was left to find an abiding place among the curios and historical memoirs of the school![14]

In some quarters, it was said that the climate in Newcastle was not good for his health, and it may be observed that Bishop's House in those days faced the cold sea at Tynemouth (the address—Front Street—speaks volumes!), but in reality the job of bishop was one he had never sought, didn't want and couldn't do. In many ways, we may consider his resignation as the most honourable thing to do.

He was awarded a generous pension from the diocese, and he returned to Rome, being appointed as the Titular Archbishop of Nicosia. He spent his remaining days in Rome and Florence. It would seem that he tried to go back to live at the Venerable English College, but Dr Giles, who had succeeded him, would not, quite sensibly, permit it. We may imagine that O'Callaghan helped out here and there, performed a few ordinations from time to time, but again very little is known of this period of his life.

Eventually he suffered a stroke that paralysed the right side of his body, and he went into the LCM home in Florence. The Little Company of Mary was founded by the Venerable Mother Mary Potter at Hyson Green in Nottingham, on 2 July 1877. The LCM is essentially a nursing order with a special charism of caring and praying for those who are dying. Originally the company existed by diocesan right, but Bishop Edward Bagshawe (1829-1913), Bishop of Nottingham at the time, was prone to interfere, even meddle, with the plans of the new order, and he did much to thwart the vision and intentions of the visionary Mother Mary. In the end, and having been diagnosed with cancer, Mother Mary went to Rome with two of her sisters in September 1882. In Rome, Pope

Leo XIII recognized the new young order and approved its rule. When Mother Mary professed her intention to return to England, he invited her to stay in Rome. It was in Rome that LCM established a hospital, called Calvary Hospital, and a training school for nurses in Via S. Stefano Rotondo. Mother Mary's health improved in Italy, and she lived until 9 April 1913 and was buried in Rome. She was declared 'Venerable' on 8 February 1988 and her mortal remains were returned to Nottingham and interred in the cathedral.

As the company expanded, Mother Mary was, in 1886, invited to establish a nursing foundation in Florence. On 18 November, "Mary Potter and sisters took up residence at Villa San Girolamo, a fifteenth-century building, and opened a noviciate and convalescent home. This building gave unrivalled views of the entire Arno Valley and of Florence with its majestic Duomo and Campanile."[15]

It was to this convalescent home that Archbishop O'Callaghan came towards the end of his life. He was unable to say Mass himself, but he had a room near the chapel and was taken to Mass each day in his wheelchair. It is said that he was very patient, made no complaints and that his rosary was scarcely out of his hands. He died at the LCM care home on 11 October 1904, aged seventy-seven. He was buried in the San Miniato al Monte cemetery in Florence. His tombstone is described as undistinguished and untended. It reads:

D.O.M.
HIC IN PACE QUIESCIT
HENRICUS O'CALLAGHAN
ORIUNDUS EX HIBERNIA LONDINI NATUS
CONGREGATIONIS OBLATORUM S. CAROLI
VENERABILIS COLLEGII ANGLORUM DE URBE
PLUSQUAM XX ANNOS RECTOR
SUMMI PONTIFICIS LEONIS XIII PRAELATUS DOMESTICUS
EPISCOPUS PRIMUM HAGULSTADENSIS ET NOVOCASTRENSIS
DEINDE ARCHIEPISCOPUS TIT. NICOSIENSIS
PARALYSI CORREPTUS INTEGRUM FERE LUSTRUM
VIM MORBI PATIENTISSIME SUSTINENS
SEPTUAGESIMO SEPTIMO ANNO MAJOR

PIE OBIIT
V ID. OCTOBRIS
MCMIV

Perhaps ironically, although he was the shortest-serving Bishop of Hexham and Newcastle and he was the only bishop not to take up permanent residence in the diocese, he was also the only one (thus far) to be raised to the rank of archbishop.

Notes

1. Charles Hart, *The Early Story of St Cuthbert's Grammar School* (London: Burns & Oates, 1941), p. 100.
2. Michael J. Walsh, *The Westminster Cardinals* (London: Burns & Oates, 2008), p. 64.
3. Ibid., p. 41.
4. See ibid., p. 65.
5. Anthony Kenny, *A Path from Rome* (London: Sidgwick and Jackson, 1985), p. 53.
6. Ibid.
7. See Michael Williams, *The Venerable English College Rome* (Leominster: Gracewing, 1979, 2008), p. 151.
8. Thomas Curtis Hayward, "College Rectors–VIII", *The Venerabile* XVI:4 (1954), pp. 215–31, here at p. 223.
9. Ibid., p. 224.
10. Williams, *The Venerable English College Rome*, p. 175.
11. Walsh, *Westminster Cardinals*, p. 70.
12. Williams, *The Venerable English College Rome*, p. 228.
13. Hart, *The Early Story of St Cuthbert's Grammar School*, p. 100.
14. See ibid., p. 101.
15. Anita MacDonald, *In the Footsteps of Venerable Mary Potter: Italy, 1882–1913* (London: LCM, 2005), p. 21.

5

Thomas William Wilkinson (1889–1909)

As we saw in the previous chapter, it was the sheer reluctance and perhaps genuine inability of Bishop O'Callaghan to run his diocese that propelled Canon Wilkinson to the fore. If Bishop O'Callaghan was unusual among his brother bishops, then so too was Wilkinson. He was appointed vicar general in early 1888, auxiliary bishop later the same year, and was translated to be diocesan bishop in 1889, the only Bishop of Hexham and Newcastle who was a former Anglican clergyman. For twenty years, he served as both bishop of the diocese and president of the diocesan seminary at Ushaw, and despite something of a midlife health crisis he lived until he was eighty-four, the longest-lived, and indeed the second-longest serving, of all the bishops of Hexham and Newcastle.

Thomas Wilkinson was born on 5 April 1825 at Harperley Park, Stanley, in County Durham. Harperley is an ancient seat and the original manor house was at Low Harperley, but Marmaduke Cradock built a new mansion on higher ground and called it Harperley Hall. In 1817, the heiress of the hall, Elizabeth Jane Pearson (through whom Bishop Wilkinson could trace his descent back to King Edward III), married George Hutton Wilkinson (d. 1859), a Cambridge and Lincoln's Inn-educated barrister from Stockton who would go on to be Deputy Lieutenant of County Durham, Recorder of Newcastle (1834) and the first County Court Judge of Northumberland (1847). He was also the first chairman of Weardale Railway, and he had his own private railway station on the Harperley estate!

George Wilkinson and his wife Elizabeth, who were married on 16 September 1817 at St Philip and St James Church, Witton-le-Wear, had six daughters and five sons, including Thomas William. From an early age, he showed an interest in farming and other country pursuits, but, aged thirteen, he was sent to Harrow School (founded 1572) for his education. Two years later, at his own request, he returned to his native North-East and then went on to the recently established University of Durham, matriculating at University College, Durham in Michaelmas term 1841. He graduated with a BA degree on 29 April 1845 and received a Licence in Theology (LTh) on 18 June 1845.[1] At about the same time, he received Holy Orders in the Church of England and was ordained priest. From Durham, Wilkinson went to the Anglo-Catholic and semi-monastic community of St Saviour, Leeds. This church had just been built to a design by the architect John Macduff Derick and had been anonymously funded by Edward Pusey, a prominent figure within the Oxford Movement. The church was established as a notable centre of Anglo-Catholicism.

It is widely recognized that the Oxford Movement began on 14 July 1833 when John Keble preached the Assize sermon in St Mary's (University) Church, Oxford on "National Apostasy". Meriol Trevor, one of Newman's biographers, wrote, "essentially the Movement was the rediscovery of the Church as an autonomous community organically one with the first disciples of Christ".[2] In particular, the English Church of the early nineteenth century was "closely enmeshed with the nation and its rulers",[3] and the bishops were more closely associated with the Tory Party than the College of the Apostles!

Additionally, Newman, who was not a central protagonist of the Oxford Movement like Pusey and Keble but was on the periphery, considered the modern Church's origins to be patristic rather than medieval, and this drew him and the Oxford Movement more widely into a more sacramental understanding of church life.

An unintended consequence of this, and of various other developments within the Church of England, especially the later Gorham Judgement of 1850, was that, rather than provoke renewal in the Church of England, it prompted many in the Church to cross the Tiber to Rome. I am always amused by the story that when Newman declared his belief that the Church of Rome was the universal (i.e. the true Catholic) Church, Henry Edward Manning, the then Anglican Archdeacon of Chichester, wrote in a letter to Gladstone that this utterance made him reel like a drunken man, and if this thought became widely known, then Newman would be disgraced and the Oxford Movement discredited.[4] The irony, of course, is that Manning himself eventually converted to Rome and went on to be the second Cardinal Archbishop of Westminster.

Within just eighteen months of being at St Saviour's, Wilkinson and his colleagues there were (on 29 December 1846) received into the Catholic Church by Fr Henry Walmsley of St Anne's, Leeds. Wilkinson's family and his father in particular, one of the most "orthodox of Protestants",[5] whilst saddened by events, did not exclude his son from the family, recognizing the purity of his intentions. A number of letters from the time, from Wilkinson's father, exist in the archives at Ushaw, and they express a father's affection for his son. A little later, Wilkinson went to the seminary at Oscott for two years. On 23 December 1848, he was ordained a priest for the Northern District in the chapel at Ushaw by Bishop William Hogarth.

He was then sent to be a missionary at the Tow Law Mission in Weardale, south of Consett. Tow Law was a rapidly expanding part of Durham at that time, following the establishment of the Weardale Iron and Coal Company in 1845. In addition to collieries, there were also blast furnaces for smelting iron, and there was a considerable expansion of the population on account of the new workforce. In the early days, Mass seems to have been celebrated at a house in the High Street. Later, in 1860, a chapel was built, which became the origin of the current parish church of St Joseph.

In 1849, Wilkinson established a mission at Wolsingham. Originally, Mass was celebrated in a rented house, but a plot of land with a hay loft and stables was purchased and a chapel, dedicated to St Thomas of Canterbury, and school were established. In 1853, building started of a new church designed by Joseph Hanson, which opened on 5 September 1854. It was dedicated by the Bishop of Hexham, Bishop Hogarth, and people attended from all over the dale.

Wilkinson also established a mission at Crook and another church by Pugin, part-funded by the parish priest, Fr Richard Ward, was built there between 1853 and 1854 and opened on 25 October 1854. The church was dedicated to Our Lady and St Cuthbert. Ward became ill and was replaced by Fr Seaton Rooke, who remained there until 1859, when he left the parish to join the Dominican Order, and Wilkinson was sent to

Crook. He was remembered there as an energetic and much-loved priest and pastor. He encouraged the Sisters of Charity to found a house in Crook to assist in the school, and the nuns arrived in 1862.

In 1865, in recognition of all his work, Wilkinson was appointed canon of the chapter of the newly created diocese of Hexham and Newcastle. In 1869, aged forty-four, Wilkinson stood down as parish priest on account of his health, having suffered something of a breakdown. Later he would write that his retirement "was ordered by a very eminent physician in London".[6] He bought a farm at Thistleflatt from some of his relatives and retired there, spending his days managing the estate. In particular, he specialized in the rearing of Durham short-horns—a pedigree breed of cattle. His diary from the time reveals a considerable grasp of agricultural technicalities.

During this time, Wilkinson kept in touch with the diocesan chapter, sometimes attending its meetings, and he also visited Ushaw and became a close friend of the then president, Dr Robert Tate.

When Bishop Bewick died on 29 October 1886, the chapter appointed Provost Edward Consitt as vicar capitular and recommended him to succeed Bewick. As I have mentioned, Rome decided otherwise, and in fact Consitt himself died very shortly afterwards in July 1887. The chapter then elected Wilkinson to the position of vicar capitular. As we know, Henry O'Callaghan was then installed as Bishop of Hexham and Newcastle in March 1888, whereupon he appointed Canon Wilkinson as provost and vicar general to administer the affairs of the diocese. A letter of congratulation to Wilkinson from his brother dated 27 May 1888, preserved in the archive at Ushaw, assures Wilkinson that he "should have no apprehension of being unequal to the charge".

O'Callaghan returned to Rome some ten weeks after his enthronement in Newcastle and subsequently, on 5 June 1888, Wilkinson was appointed Titular Bishop of Cisamus and Auxiliary Bishop of Hexham and Newcastle. He was ordained bishop at Ushaw on 25 July by Bishop William Clifford (Clifton diocese), assisted by Archbishop Charles Eyre (Glasgow) and Bishop Arthur Riddell (Northampton). Bishop O'Callaghan is conspicuous by his absence.

Bishop O'Callaghan resigned his see the following year (1889), and Wilkinson was translated to be the fifth Bishop of Hexham and Newcastle.

Nine months later, Dr James Lennon, who had been less than efficient in the role of the eleventh president of Ushaw, resigned on the grounds of poor health. As this was the second resignation within two years, the board of governors of the college requested that the new bishop take charge of the college (initially for twelve months). Wilkinson accepted this invitation at the October 1890 board meeting and took up residence at the college, living there as president until the end of his life twenty years later.

In the first instance, Ushaw's finances needed to be placed on a secure footing. Wilkinson's previous experience both in parishes and no doubt on his farm paid off and his "aptitude [for this particular task] amounted to near genius".[7] He introduced a properly recognized system of bookkeeping and employed a lay clerk to assist in the handling of accounts. He brought his farming experience to bear on the management of Ushaw's farm, and also appointed procurators and prefects to ensure the efficient day-to-day running of the college. This careful financial management enabled repairs, alterations and indeed extensions of the buildings of the college to be carried out. In particular, new dormitories were built, and a new sanitary block and modern gas-lighting were installed. Later, a cricket pavilion, a gymnasium and even a swimming pool were added.

On a separate front, it was Wilkinson who established the close links between Ushaw and Durham University, of which he was a graduate. Suitable students at Ushaw were encouraged to attend lectures at Durham and some even sat for Durham degrees. "Five times in seven years students from Ushaw took the University Classical Scholarship."[8] Furthermore, the students who studied at Durham helped to improve the academic attainment at Ushaw too, returning as minor professors and raising the standard of studies.

In 1894, approaching his seventieth birthday and exhausted by all his labours, Wilkinson wrote to Cardinal Vaughan begging him to supplicate with the Holy See that he (Wilkinson) might be allowed to resign. He points out that, for some years, "locomotion has been difficult for me" and that he would not be a financial burden to the diocese having "ample private means of my own".[9] No doubt because of all his successes, his resignation request was not granted, and Vaughan recommended that

Wilkinson seek additional assistance in the form of a co-adjutor bishop. The recommendation was transmitted to Wilkinson in a letter from Rome which began, "Most Illustrious and Most Reverend Lord!" The Pope made him an Assistant at the Pontifical Throne, and Newcastle upon Tyne granted him the Freedom of the City. Some years later he was granted an auxiliary bishop to assist him. Richard Preston, professor of moral theology at Ushaw (see below), was appointed and ordained bishop, at Ushaw, in 1900.

This must have been a great relief to Wilkinson, but he would have been disappointed when, less than five years later, Preston resigned and died soon after. He was replaced as auxiliary by Canon Richard Collins, the administrator at Newcastle Cathedral. The assistance of a new auxiliary allowed Wilkinson to devote himself to his final task: the preparations for the celebration of the centenary of Ushaw in 1908. The record in Milburn's *History of Ushaw College* is worth quoting in full:

> The centenary celebrations occupied three full days at the end of July 1908, during which time Ushaw welcomed four hundred visitors, among them Archbishop Bourne of Westminster (for some years a student at the college) and eleven bishops. Pontifical Masses in the chapel newly decorated for the occasion, dinners, speeches, a special play commissioned from Robert Hugh Benson dealing with the story of John Boste, one of the Douai priests, who worked in the vicinity of the college in the reign of Elizabeth, and the other customary trappings of English centenaries filled these few days. The president rallied sufficiently to be able to assist at almost every function, a frail and bowed but venerable prelate of eighty-three.[10]

Pope Pius X sent a message of congratulations to Wilkinson and the whole Ushaw community.

In December 1908, Wilkinson celebrated the diamond jubilee of his priestly ordination in the very chapel where he was ordained, but by that time he was really very frail. He was anointed in the first few days of March 1909 and died peacefully the following month, on 17 April 1909. Many telegrams and letters of condolence were sent to Mgr Joseph

Corbishley (who succeeded Wilkinson as college president) at Ushaw following Wilkinson's death, and they are a testament to the high regard in which the bishop was held by so many. Bishop John Baptist Cahill of Portsmouth wrote to excuse himself from the funeral but remarked that his associations with Wilkinson were always most pleasant.

In his funeral Mass homily, the Very Revd John Norris D.D. commended all the work Wilkinson had done at Ushaw, improving the material fabric of the place and its intellectual and formative programme. Through his work at the college, Wilkinson had served the whole diocese. Moreover, Norris praised the

> spirit which the Bishop diffused through the whole house—a spirit of unity and peace, a spirit of serious earnestness of purpose, a spirit of greater gentleness and consideration, a spirit of sympathetic relationship, a spirit of wider outlook and greater breadth of thought. Above all—supremely above all—how carefully he fostered and nurtured the spirit of real piety which he found already flourishing when he came.[11]

Following the liturgical formalities, Wilkinson was buried at Ushaw, which had been his home for so long. A plaque in the cemetery cloister there refers to his lifetime of working for God, describing him as prudent and peace-making and referring to his ardent faith in the Lord (*fide ardens in Domino*). Bishop Wilkinson left his entire estate, a fortune of over £50,000, to Ushaw College for the education of priests in the county of Durham, which he had loved so much.

Notes

1. Data provided by Durham University Archives and Special Collections.
2. Meriol Trevor, *Newman's Journey* (Glasgow: Collins, 1974), p. 55.
3. Ibid., p. 57.
4. See ibid., p. 106.
5. David Milburn, *A History of Ushaw College* (Ushaw: 1964), p. 296.
6. Letter quoted in ibid., p. 301.
7. Ibid., p. 299.
8. Ibid., p. 304.
9. Ibid., p. 301.
10. Ibid., p. 307.
11. Ibid., p. 308.

5 A

Richard Preston (1900–4)

Richard Preston was born on 12 December 1856 at St Leonard's Gate, Lancaster, the son of Richard Preston and his wife Helen née Wilson. He had at least two brothers, one of whom, Joseph (1859–89), although short-lived, was a priest. Like his brother, he was schooled at Ushaw, firstly at the junior seminary, and David Milburn records that he arrived in 1864, aged only eight or nine.[1] He was serious-minded, intent on being a priest, and was remembered as having a dominant character and an ability for games. He could also draw and would often take a pencil to while away spare time. He remained at Ushaw until 1881, by which time he would have been twenty-five and would have completed all of his schooling and ("undergraduate") studies.

He was then sent to the Venerable English College in Rome (where Henry O'Callaghan was then rector) for further studies and was ordained priest for the Liverpool diocese by Cardinal Lucido Maria Parocchi (1833–1903) in St John Lateran, Rome, on 7 June 1884.[2] He is recorded as a Doctor of Divinity (DD), and we may presume that these studies were completed in Rome. He is also said to have spent some time at the University of Innsbruck in Austria,[3] and we can assume that these studies equipped him for his subsequent return to Ushaw to teach.

He returned to Ushaw in 1886 and remained there as professor of scripture and later moral theology[4] until 1900, when he was appointed auxiliary bishop to Bishop Wilkinson.

On 25 July 1900, he was ordained Titular Bishop of Phocaea and auxiliary of Hexham and Newcastle in the chapel at Ushaw. The principal consecrator was Bishop Thomas William Wilkinson, assisted by Bishop (later Archbishop) Thomas Whiteside (the first Bishop of Liverpool) and Bishop Francis Joseph Mostyn (b. 1860, first Bishop of Menevia), not to be confused with Francis George Mostyn (b. 1800), one time Vicar Apostolic of the Northern District.

Bishop Preston, a scholar by nature, was a reluctant bishop. At Christmas, after his episcopal ordination, he wrote to a friend:

> This being a bishop, even in the mitigated auxiliary form is I assure you very terrible—it is very sad that your only qualification for office is an overwhelming consciousness of your utter unfitness for it.[5]

The first challenge for the new bishop was the Catholic Congress held in Newcastle in 1901. The first national Catholic Congress had been held in Leeds the previous year, and the second took place in Newcastle, focusing particularly on education. Without going into detail, the reports in *The Tablet* (12 August 1901) give us some idea of what went on. There was: the Lord Mayor's banquet, Sunday in the churches, a sermon by the Bishop of Newport, a mass meeting of women, a speech by Professor Windle, Mr Belloc's view, sectional meetings etc. There was no end of distinguished visitors, including Cardinal Vaughan:

> On the Wednesday afternoon of the Congress a garden Fête was held in Jesmond Dene, presided over by our newly consecrated auxiliary bishop, Dr Richard Preston ... [and] ... the grand finale of the Congress was the mass meeting held in the White City. That evening the hall was crowded to its utmost capacity. Dr Preston presided ...[6]

It must have been quite a challenge for a new bishop, but it appears he excelled in the task.

As well as continuing his teaching duties during the week, Bishop Preston undertook many diocesan duties on Bishop Wilkinson's behalf at the weekends, touring the diocese, visiting churches and confirming. On 23 July 1904, Preston laid the foundation stone at Our Lady and St Cuthbert's Church, Prudhoe. Prudhoe developed as a mining town in the late nineteenth century and there was originally a mission based at Prudhoe Hall. When the hall was sold, the chapel was moved. Charles

Walker of Newcastle was the architect for this move and a school and a teacher's house were also built. Auxiliary Bishop Collins (see below) opened the new church on 5 October 1905.

Preston's visits to St Cuthbert's Grammar School were also remembered with affection and give us a glimpse of his character and his humour. Fr Hart recalled:

> During the short years of his episcopacy (1900-5), his visits to the Grammar School were frequent, and always much appreciated by masters and boys alike. His beautiful and cheerful life was an inspiration to all, yet some of his words in his first episcopal address to the boys assembled to welcome him were a pleasant little leg-pulling to the budding disciples of Xenophon, Plato and Aristotle. 'I am given to understand' he told them, 'that the life of a bishop is arduous, his work unending, and at times difficult and exhausting, yet, were you to multiply all this by two, I would still face being a bishop rather than have, once again, to plod to the end of the passive voice in tupto'. And he seemed to mean it.[7]

More formally, it seems that it was Bishop Preston who initiated the periodic (quinquennial), but formal, inspection of parishes. This practice derives from Decree 29 of the Westminster Provincial Council of 1852, but does not really seem to have been adopted in the diocese of Hexham and Newcastle. The *Journal of the Catholic Archives Society* records:

> no records of any visitation in Hogarth's time (1850-66) or during Wilkinson's first thirteen years (1889-1901) survive, but there is almost a full series for 1902, perhaps carried out by Bishop Preston (1900-1905), Wilkinson's first Auxiliary. The returns are then desultory until 1925, from which date they are nearly complete.[8]

It seems more than likely to me that Preston would have recognized Wilkinson's preoccupation with the seminary and gone out of his way to visit, "inspect" and encourage the churches and clergy in the diocese.

On 22 December 1904, after fewer than five years as auxiliary bishop, Preston resigned on account of ill-health, which may have been tuberculosis. He celebrated Mass for the last time on Christmas Day. He retired to Southfield, Lancaster, the home of his brother, who had been three times Mayor of Southfield. Just a few months later, Bishop Preston died on 9 February 1905 at the early age of forty-eight. An admirer wrote: "Bishop Preston was one of those men we stand so much in need of, a scholar, a theologian, an administrator, a firm yet lovable character of deepest simplest piety."[9]

He is buried at Ushaw College.

Notes

[1] See David Milburn, *A History of Ushaw College* (Ushaw: 1964), p. 365.

[2] He is listed in the *Venerabile* magazine, May 1954, p. 225.

[3] See Brian Plumb, *Arundel to Zabi: A Biographical Dictionary of the Catholic Bishops of England and Wales (Deceased) 1623–2000* (Wigan: North West Catholic History Society, 1987, 2006), p. 172.

[4] Milburn, *A History of Ushaw College*, pp. 301 and 365.

[5] Quoted in Plumb, *Arundel to Zabi*, p. 172.

[6] C. Hart, *The Early Story of St Cuthbert's Grammar School* (London: Burns & Oates, 1941), p. 101.

[7] Ibid., p. 106.

[8] R. Gard, "The Archives of the Diocese of Hexham and Newcastle", *Catholic Archives*, 19 (1999), pp. 24–41, here at p. 33.

[9] Plumb, *Arundel to Zabi*, p. 172.

6

Richard Collins (1909–24)

When Auxiliary Bishop Preston died in 1905, Richard Collins was appointed to replace him as auxiliary. Four years later when Bishop Wilkinson died, Bishop Collins succeeded him, being translated to the diocese of Hexham and Newcastle as its sixth bishop.

Richard Collins was born on 5 April 1857 at Newbury, Berkshire, the son of Michael Collins and Marie née Martin. Three of his sisters would go on to become nuns. He received his elementary schooling at a school opened in the 1850s by the Misses Barratt, for the Catholic children of Newbury, in a rented cottage in the Rose and Thistle Yard.[1]

He went north to Ushaw, arriving there, aged only twelve, in 1869, and from the junior seminary he went up to the major seminary to study for the priesthood.[2] He was ordained priest, at Ushaw, on 30 May 1885 by Bishop Bewick. Brian Plumb records:

> For several years prior to ordination he held the office of minor professor. He had charge of a class of juniors and his reputation for being thorough rather than spectacular earned him the lifelong friendship of such searching superiors as Cardinal Bourne and Archbishop Whiteside.[3]

Francis Alphonsus Bourne (1861–1935) was at Ushaw between 1869 and 1875, although the boarding school experience was one that he did not like.[4] He was ordained for the Southwark diocese (before it became an archdiocese in 1965). He did a little parish work before becoming the first rector of the new seminary at Wonersh. He was ordained Titular Bishop of Epiphania in Cilicia and coadjutor Bishop of Southwark in 1896, succeeding to the see in 1897 at the young age of thirty-six. He was translated to be the fourth Bishop of Westminster in 1903, he was one of the guests of honour at the centenary celebration at Ushaw in 1908, and he received the cardinal's red hat in 1911. It was fitting that, as one of Collins' former seminary friends, Bourne assisted at Collins' episcopal ordination in 1905.

Thomas Whiteside (1857–1921) was at Ushaw between 1873 and 1881, and then went on to the English College in Rome, where he was ordained priest for the Liverpool diocese in 1885. He then taught at and was eventually rector of the Liverpool diocesan seminary at Upholland, before being ordained Bishop of Liverpool in 1894. When Liverpool was raised to the status of an archdiocese, in 1911, Whiteside became the first archbishop and metropolitan.

After Ushaw, Collins was sent to serve as assistant priest at the nearby mission in Newhouse. There had been a Catholic presence here from the late seventeenth century. A chapel was built in the 1730s, and a new church was opened by Bishop Chadwick in 1871. This was damaged by fire in 1881, and another church (dedicated to Our Lady Queen of Martyrs) opened in 1883. The parish priest was Fr Fortin, "the pitmen's priest", whom Collins assisted. Collins then went to St Thomas of Canterbury Church, Wolsingham, the parish (or mission) that Wilkinson, now the bishop, had established in 1849. Shortly afterwards, the neighbouring parish of Witton Park was also put into his care, and Collins established a small church there, building much of it himself. It was dedicated to St Chad and closed in 1988. These were small parishes, spread over the picturesque moorland, but were very poor and, on a very small income, Collins lived a frugal and simple life.

He then went briefly to St Joseph's, Tow Law, where the church had been opened in 1869 and the presbytery in 1872. Finally, in 1891, Collins was sent to be rector of St Andrew's Catholic Church in Newcastle. This was a busy parish at the time, and it had considerable debts, but with zeal and self-sacrifice he soon had the parish solvent. In 1895, he was appointed as administrator at the cathedral and then appointed a canon of the diocese in 1897.

On 31 March 1905, following Bishop Preston's death, Collins was appointed Titular Bishop of Selinus and Auxiliary Bishop of Hexham and Newcastle. He was ordained bishop in the cathedral on 29 June by

Archbishop Francis Bourne (Westminster), assisted by Bishop Francis Mostyn (Menevia) and Bishop George Barton (Clifton). As Bishop Wilkinson was resident at Ushaw, Bishop Collins took up residence in the Bishop's House at Tynemouth. Following the death of Bishop Wilkinson, Collins was appointed as his successor by the Holy See on 21 June 1909.

As a bishop, Collins continued to live simply and frugally, ministering to his flock. He said his daily Mass at a convent a tram ride from his house, often giving up his seat on the tram to those who had been working a nightshift. He is reported to have said, "You have been working all night. I have not." This simple attitude earned him the respect and affection of many locals.

In 1911, Canon Howe's church at Whitley Bay was finally finished. Dedicated to St Edward, who was one of Howe's particular patrons, it was designed by Edward J. Kay and Gibson's of North Shields were the architects. It was built by William Gray and is described as simple in style, the interior having an oak decor with pine pews. There were electric lights and heating pipes. The opening was, it can only be said, grand and reported by the *Shields Daily News*. Bishop Collins offered the Mass, the choir sang Gounod's *Mass of the Sacred Heart*, Miss Smith and Mr Johnson singing the solo parts and Mr Nesbitt playing the organ. Dean Haggarty, rector of St Cuthbert's, North Shields, preached the sermon on "this day is salvation come to this house" (Luke 19:9).

At the time, Whitley Bay was really a mission: Bishop Collins referred to the "new mission" in a letter to Canon Howe, dated 26 December 1910, when the boundaries of the mission were agreed. It was not until (2 February) 1918 that Whitley Bay was strictly designated as a parish and Fr Patrick Kearney was appointed as the first parish priest.

In 1912, Bishop Collins opened another new church, acquired for the diocese in somewhat unusual circumstances. St Mary's Church, North Gosforth, was built as an Anglican church in the mid-1860s under the generous patronage of Thomas Eustace Smith (1831–1903), who was from a prominent family of rope-makers and was the Liberal MP for Tynemouth between 1868 and 1885. The architect of the church is unknown, but it was built in the Early English style and contains notable stained glass by William Morris and Company, designed by Pre-Raphaelite artists including Burne-Jones, Madox Brown and Morris himself. Thomas Smith spent around £12,000 on the church, but it was never actually consecrated, as Smith was worried about losing control of the church to the diocese of Durham, a fear that was amplified by his belief that the Church of England might be disestablished.

Following the foundation of the Church of St Columba in Seaton Burn in the 1870s and the sale of the Gosforth Park Estate to the High Gosforth Park Racecourse Company in 1880, St Mary's Church went into decline and was eventually closed in the early 1900s. In 1911, the church was showing signs of disrepair and the grounds around it were overgrown. Following the death of Smith, the family of the founding MP sought to have the church reopened and approached the Church of England, but there was no interest. By contrast, Bishop Collins showed considerable interest in reopening the church and, after some negotiations, he bought it from Thomas Smith's widow for £3,000, spending his own money.

The bishop himself said the first Catholic Mass there on 28 January 1912, and on 24 June the church was formally opened and rededicated to the Sacred Heart. Bishop Collins obviously had great affection for this church and left provision for it in his will. Additionally, he left some of his own furniture and artworks for the presbytery at Sacred Heart. The diocesan archives refer to a proposal in 1930 to erect a new high altar as a memorial to Bishop Collins.

A delightfully personal recollection of Bishop Collins is provided by Fr Hart, of St Cuthbert's Grammar School. The context is the significant work that the headmaster of the school, Fr Horace Mann, had done on the popes of the Middle Ages, which resulted in his book *The Lives of the Popes of the Early Middle Ages* (1902). This was personally acknowledged by a letter to Mann from Pope Pius X in 1911, on the occasion of the silver jubilee of Mann's ordination, but more was to follow:[5]

> I think it was a Saturday morning, when soon after our return from the holidays, that our own bishop, Dr Collins, might have been seen hastening on foot up Bath Lane on his way to the school. I chanced to be in the hall when he entered, and was the first to greet him. With a happy twinkle in his eye he asked: 'Where is Dr Mann?' '*Father* Mann, I believe, is in his room.' 'Just wait a bit', he said, 'you will soon see who is right'; and he pointed

to what appeared to be an important document held in his left
hand. It turned out to be the brief from Rome conferring on our
Headmaster the honoured title of 'Doctor', a title of address which
for a long time got much confused with its 25 year old rival title
of Father. The bishop motioned me to accompany him into the
Doctor's presence.

One can still recall the look of surprise that showed itself on
the Doctor's face, and his effort to subdue his pent-up feelings.
In this he was not altogether successful, for in spite of his best
efforts, his eyes were not altogether free from tell-tale moisture.
After a few more minutes, with the Bishop seated on the *predella*
and in front of the tabernacle of our community chapel, the
new Doctor faltered out his Profession of Faith before the Holy
Father's representative. The scene was simple, but oh, how
touching![6]

In 1914, Collins would ordain two "Old Cuthbertians" to the priesthood:
Fr Joseph McElroy and Fr John Deans, who were both initially appointed
to fill positions at the school.

Perhaps the biggest challenge of Collins' episcopacy was the First
World War. A number of troops were stationed along the coast for
defensive purposes and trenches were dug on the beach at Whitley Bay.
The clergy had extra demands put upon them ministering to the military
forces. Special Masses were celebrated for the troops on Sundays, and it
had to be ensured that those who wished it had received the sacrament
before departing for France. It is reported that

> [A]lthough there was not the same threat of aerial bombardment
> that there was in the Second World War, there was nevertheless a
> real danger from the air. In August 1916, for example, a zeppelin
> cruised over Whitley Bay on a clear night and dropped bombs
> which destroyed some houses in Albany Gardens. The snuffing
> out of the Sanctuary Lamp each evening on the instruction of
> the Bishop was therefore sensible.[7]

Towards the end of his episcopacy, Collins suffered ill-health, although he managed to make his *ad limina* visit to Rome in 1922 and was received by the Pope. Later in that same year, he acted as the co-consecrator of Bishop Robert Dobson, the Auxiliary Bishop of Liverpool, but he was not a well man. His Vicar General, Canon James Rooney, had to manage much of the day-to-day administration of the diocese.

He suffered a seizure, and then a second, and died in Newcastle on 9 February 1924. Crowds queued in the sleet to file past his open coffin in the cathedral to pay their last respects. After his funeral Mass, he was buried at Ushaw.

Following Bishop Collins' death and before the installation of his successor, there was an adjustment of diocesan boundaries. By the Apostolic Constitution, *Universalis ecclesiae solicitudo*, dated 22 November 1924, Pope Pius XI erected the new diocese of Lancaster, which was created from the western part of the diocese of Hexham and Newcastle (in fact the old counties of Cumberland and Westmorland) and a portion of the archdiocese of Liverpool. The new diocese was, and is, part of the Province of Liverpool. The diocese is centred on Lancaster Cathedral, a diocesan church dedicated to St Peter, completed in 1859, which was raised to the rank of cathedral in 1924. The first bishop was Dom Thomas Pearson OSB (1870–1938). The diocese today "comprises the County of Cumbria and the Hundreds of Amounderness and Lonsdale in the County of Lancashire (north of the river Ribble)".[8] It has an area of some 2,900 square kilometres.

Notes

1. See Gerald Dwyer, *Diocese of Portsmouth–Past and Present* (Portsmouth: Portsmouth Diocesan Centenary Committee, 1981), p. 98.
2. Collins is recorded as being at Ushaw from 1869–95. David Milburn, *A History of Ushaw College* (Ushaw: 1964), p. 365.
3. Brian Plumb, *Arundel to Zabi: A Biographical Dictionary of the Catholic Bishops of England and Wales (Deceased) 1623–2000* (Wigan: North West Catholic History Society, 1987, 2006), p. 70.
4. See Michael J. Walsh, *The Westminster Cardinals* (London: Burns & Oates, 2008), p. 85.
5. See C. Hart, *The Early History of St Cuthbert's Grammar School* (London: Burns & Oates, 1941), pp. 112–13.
6. Ibid., pp. 113–14.
7. David R. Russell, *History Written for St Edward's Centenary Celebrations, 23 October 2011*, <http://www.northtynesidecatholic.org.uk/wp-content/uploads/2015/02/St-Edwards-History1.pdf>, accessed 2 November 2021, p. 4.
8. Chris Larsen, *Catholic Bishops of Great Britain* (Durham: Sacristy Press, 2016), p. 112.

7

Joseph William Thorman (1924-36)

Bishop Collins was succeeded by Bishop Thorman. In a number of different ways, Bishop Thorman's early life was, to say the least, rather unusual.

Bishop Joseph William Thorman's grandfather was a Scottish iron merchant's agent also named Joseph Thorman, recorded in the 1871 census living with his wife Jane and their son (and third child) Joseph Thomas Thorman (1847-74), a ship and chandler clerk, at 1 Leays Crescent in Newcastle. A little later, in May 1871, Joseph Thomas Thorman married Anna Mary Rennoldson (1851-1926) in Newcastle. She was the daughter of William Rennoldson (b. 1818) and Marianne née Jobling (b. 1814 or 1815).

Just a few months after this wedding, the newly-weds' first son Joseph was born, on 6 August 1871, at 67 Chichester Street, Gateshead. The bishop-to-be had a younger sister, Maud Mary Thorman, born in the third quarter of 1873. Bishop Thorman's father died in Gateshead (of an unknown cause, but most probably some accident) in 1874. No probate records are found, so he left his widow with two young children and no income. What was a mother to do?

In the 1881 census, Joseph William Thorman, then aged nine, is recorded as "an inmate" at Moor Edge Orphanage. Also known as the Northern Counties Orphan Institute, and originally situated in West Clayton Street in Newcastle, it was founded by the Revd J. Lintott in 1864 to "maintain, clothe and educate fatherless, and in exceptional cases, motherless children of indigent circumstances".[1] As a charitable institution, it seems to have been fairly well endowed, and in 1867 a foundation stone was laid for a new building on the edge of Town Moor, beside the Deaf and Dumb Institute. The Abbot Memorial Building included a large and lofty dining room, schoolroom and classrooms, along with a teachers' room and kitchen etc. on the ground floor. The first floor contained dormitories; hot and cold baths and lavatories were conveniently situated. Externally, the building looked like a Jacobean-style mansion. Although it was an orphanage, and not a workhouse, and the boy would have been reasonably well looked after, the nine-year-old Joseph cannot have enjoyed being separated from his mother and his sister.

The same 1881 census records the bishop's mother as Anna M. Reynolds (a spelling error), working as a governess at 28 Lorraine Place in Newcastle, for the family of Anton G. Shaeffer and his wife, Isabella née Lambert (b. 1827). Anton Shaeffer (1834–1903) was a German-born, naturalized British subject, who was a consulting marine engineer originally from Koblenz. Perhaps the most significant thing about him, for our story, is that he was a Catholic. As was customary at the time, he was baptized on the day after his birth and the records for 4 February (1834) have an entry for one Antonius Georgius Shaeffer.

In the first quarter of 1882, Frau Shaeffer died and, after a suitable interval and in *The Sound of Music* style, Herr Shaeffer married his governess (now recorded as Anna Mary Thorman) in June 1883. They went on to have three children, Bishop Thorman's half-siblings: Paul (b. 1884), Marie (b. 1886) and Anton (b. 1889). Presumably at this stage, young Joseph was "rescued" from the orphanage and returned to live with his mother, sister, stepfather and, in due course, his half-siblings. When Anton Shaeffer died in December 1903, probate records list his effects as £5,088 9s 10d, so we can infer that the family was reasonably "well off".

It is recorded that Joseph was received into the Roman Catholic Church on 24 October 1885 and baptized at St Anthony's Church, Walker. He went to study at St Cuthbert's Grammar School in Newcastle before going on to Ushaw to study for the priesthood in 1888, aged seventeen. Thorman is recorded as having matriculated at London University as an external Ushaw student in 1890, but he does not appear to have graduated with a London degree. He was ordained priest at Ushaw on 27 September 1896 by Bishop Wilkinson.

After his ordination, he was appointed as assistant priest at St Mary's Cathedral, where he remained for three years which were interspersed with brief periods of supply at St Joseph's, Tow Law and St Thomas of Canterbury, Wolsingham.

In 1889, he was appointed rector of St Patrick's Church, Langley Moor, Durham. This was a colliery parish which was originally founded in 1876 to serve the Irish migrant community who had arrived to work in the mines. The mission was based at a house in the High Street which served as the presbytery and where Mass was originally celebrated. In 1879, a new zinc church was built, and in 1885 a new presbytery too. Fr Richard Hannon, the second rector, also bought additional land in 1884.

Fr Thorman was the third rector, and he built a school attached to the church for 307 children. It exists to this day and is described as a small Catholic primary school which provides a safe, caring and nurturing environment. Thorman also laid important plans for the building of a new church, but the money had to be raised first. In the end, it was his successor as rector who in 1910 laid the foundation stone of the new church, which was formally opened on Sunday 8 October 1911. High Mass was offered by Mgr Brown, the president of Ushaw College, and Fr Thorman acted as the sub-deacon.

In 1906, Thorman was transferred to St Andrew's Church, Worswick Street, an industrial parish in the centre of Newcastle. The 1911 census records him living with two younger priests and three female domestic servants. The church was built in 1875, replacing an earlier building (the first post-Reformation Catholic church in Newcastle) in Pilgrim Street, built by Fr James Worswick (d. 1843). At the time the church faced various problems: it had a large debt and was at least threatened with demolition as part of the project to build a new bridge across the Tyne.

During the First World War, Thorman organized relief for Belgian refugees and was awarded the Order of King Leopold, the oldest and highest Belgian order named after King Leopold I for meritorious service to the Belgian state or society.[2] Characteristically, Thorman himself was very modest about this. While at St Andrew's, Thorman was an ardent cyclist and during his summer holiday spent his time cycling to the cathedrals of England.

A very human vignette is recalled by Fr Hart, whose book on St Cuthbert's Grammar School has been frequently quoted in this text and who, after a lifetime of teaching, was ordained to the priesthood, aged fifty-nine. Hart wrote:

> Father Joseph Thorman, P.P. of St Andrew's, one of our old boys and soon to be bishop, said, very touchingly, 'I have longed to call you "Father", now I can do so and if I may, I would like to serve one of your first Masses.' This he did at St Andrew's on the Tuesday morning when for the first time the young priest (59 years old) used at the altar the handsome silver chalice presented to him by his old boy priests.[3]

Following the death of Bishop Collins in January 1924, Thorman was appointed the seventh Bishop of Hexham and Newcastle on 18 December 1924 and ordained bishop on 27 January the following year at the hands of Archbishop Frederick Keating (Liverpool), assisted by Bishop Joseph Cowgill (Leeds) and Bishop Thomas Dunn (Nottingham). Thorman took the episcopal motto *Servitor Maneo*, "I remain a servant".

As bishop, Thorman was involved in founding or opening a number of new churches and schools, which were established in the optimism of the inter-war years and did much to consolidate the diocese. In 1926, Bishop Thorman opened All Saints' Church, Lanchester. The parish was founded in 1901 from the mother church of St Michael's, Esh Laude, and a school was opened. The original tin chapel was replaced in 1926 by a new church built to the design of a Bavarian architect, Theo Korner, at a cost of £4,500. The Italian marble in the sanctuary came from the Regent Hotel in the Strand! The church was formally opened by Bishop Thorman on 3 November.

In 1927, he laid the foundation stone for a new school at St Patrick's Church, Felling. The original "old St Patrick's church" was built in 1842 on Felling shore. A new church was planned by Fr John Kelly and begun in 1872, but difficulties at the site and the cost delayed the work. It was not until Fr Murphy arrived in 1892 that developments got underway again. A new school was opened in 1893 and the new church, designed by Charles Walker of Newcastle, was completed in 1895. It was opened by Bishop Wilkinson on St Patrick's Day, 17 March. It has been described as "the glory of Felling, and the admiration of the visitor, [it] is a basilica of the Romanesque style".[4] As the communities grew, a new school was required and St Alban's School was opened, the foundation stone of which was laid by Bishop Thorman in 1927.

On 23 April 1928, Thorman blessed and opened the new church of St Edward, Whitley Bay. Designed by architects Stienlet and Maxwell, this new church replaced the earlier 1910 church, which the community had outgrown, but which became the parish hall and the centre for much parish activity. High Mass was celebrated by Bishop Thorman, assisted by Fr James Farrow of St Mary's Cathedral and Fr John Corby of Sunderland. The choir from the seminary provided the music and Fr George Whitley preached. After Mass, there was a lunch at the Waverley Hotel (now the Rex Hotel), and in the evening the bishop led a solemn benediction.[5]

I think the proximity of the new church to the bishop's residence in Front Street, Tynemouth, may go some way to explaining the celebrations. Following the opening of the church, it was subsequently consecrated:

> At a subsequent celebration of Pontifical High Mass the church was filled to overflowing. Following the impressively dignified ceremony of the outside walls of the building, during which the Bishop sprinkled the walls with holy water, the Litany of the Saints was sung at the entrance, and the Bishop's procession entered the church. The interior walls were also blessed by his Lordship in the presence of the congregation. The preparations for Mass were only exceeded in inspiring dignity and ceremonial by the celebration of the service itself. The Bishop in his scarlet Pontifical robes had the assistance of several scarlet-robed priests, who included Fathers Farrow, Kinleside, Curry, Cronin, McClean, Thompson, Scurr, Wilkinson, Watson, Madden and Pippet.[6]

In 1932, Thorman dedicated the new school at St Agnes' Parish, Crawcrook. The original school was established in the late 1880s and a chapel was added in 1892. A temporary church with an iron roof was built in 1905. A bigger school was established and blessed by Thorman in 1932, but this in turn eventually moved to the larger site of the former

Kepier Chare Primary School. The former school became a Catholic club, but was eventually demolished, and houses now stand on the site.

Additionally, while Thorman was bishop, a number of religious houses were opened in the diocese. The Jesuits opened a retreat house in Sunderland, the Mill Hill Fathers came to Croxdale, and the convent of the Helpers of the Holy Souls opened in South Shields. In total, thirty-five Mass centres were begun, many of which developed into parishes, and fifteen churches were consecrated. Despite all these achievements, Thorman was neither puffed-up nor proud. "My clergy always do what I suggest" was one of his familiar expressions and speaks volumes about his approach.

In 1928, Thorman was appointed president of the Catholic Social Guild (CSG), succeeding Archbishop Keating, and is described as a "notable Guild activist and supporter".[7] The CSG was founded in September 1909, in Manchester, by a group of priests and laymen. The stated purpose of the guild was "to promote the study of social questions in the light of the teaching of the Catholic Church; to spread the knowledge of the principles and of practical conclusions; to prepare all who will take a more active part in the social apostolate." Membership was open to all Catholics. A Catholic workers' college, called Plater College, was established in Oxford in 1921.

The guild produced many publications on Catholic social action, and in particular under Thorman's presidency: "A Code of Social Principles" (1929), "Catholic Social Action 1891–1931" (1933), and the 1931 papal encyclical *Quadragesimo Anno* on Catholic social teaching was also given considerable publicity. Additionally, the guild produced a quarterly bulletin and a monthly periodical, *The Christian Democrat*. Thorman remained president until his death in 1936. In the minutes of the annual meeting, held on 1 August 1937 at Ruskin College, Oxford, the secretary reported:

> It pleased God to call Bishop Joseph Thorman to his reward after eight years of devoted and efficient direction as our President, and so soon after his presence at our last Annual Meeting gave us hope that he had been restored to health. He followed the affairs of the Guild and the proceedings of our committee

with the keenest interest and sympathy, always encouraging, advising wisely, inspiring confidence. Ever ready to help, praying constantly and urging prayer for God's blessing on our work.[8]

In the light of his own childhood, it is fitting, and indeed poignant, that in 1929 Thorman founded the Children's Care and Homes Committee for children who were destitute and in danger of losing their faith. The children were cared for in four homes at Newcastle, Gainford, Tudhoe and Darlington. In a Lenten pastoral letter, Thorman pointed out that, although the 1911 Children and Young Persons Act provided safeguards for the religion of a child, there was "no Catholic approved school in the diocese to which Catholic children could be sent under the provision of the act".[9] Similarly, although there were "poor homes" in the area provided by the 1930 Poor Law Act, there was no specifically Catholic provision.

Thorman's committee proposed remedies to this situation and the bishop exhorted clergy and laity alike to co-operate with the committee to improve the prospects for Catholic children. There was a certain amount of political wrangling between Thorman's committee and the local authorities, and the issues were even raised in Parliament, but eventually Catholic children were transferred from municipal provision to Catholic children's homes.

By 1935, Thorman's health had begun to decline, but he bore a painful illness with exemplary patience. During a period of respite, he wrote to the secretary of the guild: "By the goodness of God I am back at my altar," which I read as a telling and significant utterance of a churchman, contrasting sharply with its more modern counterpart—"back at my desk".

Thorman made an *ad limina* visit to Rome and was received by Pope Pius XI, but he was very ill on his return. In June, he spent some time in hospital and, although he made something of a recovery, eventually he had to return to the Minories hospital of the Dominican sisters in Newcastle. Before finally leaving his Bishop's House in Tynemouth, he put his affairs in order and wrote a note saying: "Now I owe no man anything, except perhaps anyone I have injured or neglected."[10]

Bishop Thorman died on 7 October 1936 (aged sixty-five) at St Catherine's Nursing Home, Jesmond Road, Newcastle. Probate records show effects of £314 8s left to Frs George McBrierty and Hugh McCartan. Thorman's Requiem Mass was celebrated by Archbishop Downey, Archbishop of Liverpool, in Newcastle Cathedral, which was packed to capacity. Five further bishops and some 300 priests also attended, not to mention civic dignitaries and ordinary people. The Bishop of Nottingham, John Francis McNulty, preached the homily. He likened Bishop Thorman to St Cuthbert, of whom it was written by his biographer, "the events of his career are few and mostly hidden". As an *alter Christus* Thorman gave his life to the service of God. His work was always done quietly, efficiently and without fuss.

> After Mass the funeral procession passed between kneeling crowds and proceeded on its way to Ushaw College where the burial was to take place. As the cortège passed through the villages en route, small groups that had gathered in the main streets paid a last farewell to the bishop whom they all loved. Here and there were bands of pitmen, whose begrimed faces showed they had just left work, standing cap-in-hand as the procession passed. The little children too, allowed away from their lessons for a few minutes, lined up by the roadside and added their sweet innocent prayers to the supplications of a sorrowing diocese.[11]

He was buried at Ushaw alongside his predecessor, Bishop Collins. A memorial plaque in the cemetery cloister there describes him as a man of ability and prudence (*vir ingenio et prudentia*).

Notes

1. See <http://www.childrenshomes.org.uk/NewcastleOrphanage/>, accessed 8 December 2021.
2. See Brian Plumb, *Arundel to Zabi: A Biographical Dictionary of the Catholic Bishops of England and Wales (Deceased) 1623–2000* (Wigan: North West Catholic History Society, 1987, 2006), p. 194.
3. Charles Hart, *The Early Story of St Cuthbert's Grammar School* (London: Burns & Oates, 1941), p. 117.
4. Tom R. Sterling, *The History of St Patrick's RC Church, Felling, 1895–2014* (2014), <http://www.stpatricks-felling.co.uk/wp-content/uploads/The-history-of-St-Patricks-Booklet-1.pdf>, accessed 2 November 2021, p. 24.
5. See *The Universe*, 27 April 1928, quoted in David R. Russell, *History Written for St Edward's Centenary Celebrations, 23 October 2011*, <http://www.northtynesidecatholic.org.uk/wp-content/uploads/2015/02/St-Edwards-History1.pdf>, accessed 2 November 2021.
6. Russell, *History Written for St Edward's Centenary Celebrations*, p. 5.
7. R. Gard, "Societies II", *Catholic Archives* 22 (2002), pp. 26–34, here at p. 31.
8. *The Catholic Social Guild, Report of the Twenty-Eighth Annual Meeting*, p. 2.
9. *Catholic Herald*, 16 March 1935.
10. Plumb, *Arundel to Zabi*, p. 194.
11. *Catholic Herald*, 18 October 1936.

8

Joseph McCormack (1937–58)

Bishop Joseph McCormack is distinguished as being the longest-serving Bishop of Hexham and Newcastle, ruling the diocese faithfully for twenty-one years (1937–58), in a period characterized by "steady growth and development".[1] He was bishop throughout the difficult years of the Second World War and the years that immediately followed it.

Joseph McCormack was born on 17 May 1887 at Broadway in Worcestershire. His parents were Joseph McCormack and Honora née Graham. The family moved to Tyneside and young McCormack and his brothers attended St Cuthbert's Grammar School, Newcastle.

He was described as a student of ability and promise and, along with his brother John, proceeded to Ushaw in 1905, where he passed with marked success through the schools of philosophy and theology.[2] Whereas John completed his studies in Rome and returned to Ushaw as a professor, Joseph remained at Ushaw and was ordained priest there, for the diocese of Hexham and Newcastle, on 11 August 1912.

McCormack was appointed by Bishop Collins as his secretary, a post he held for almost fifteen years. As has been said before, the post of bishop's secretary is often seen as an apprenticeship for the role of bishop itself and, during these years as Bishop Collins' secretary, McCormack would have learnt much about the diocese and the role of bishop.

In 1927, McCormack was sent to the new parish church of St Teresa of the Infant Jesus, Heaton, as the first parish priest. There had been a Catholic community in Heaton since the start of the 1920s. In 1927, a presbytery was bought in Simonside Terrace and Fr McCormack began celebrating Mass in a flat or maisonette on Heaton Road. Subsequently, land was bought and a small church, affectionately known as "the tin hut", was built, and in 1932 a new presbytery beside it.

In 1929, McCormack was appointed vicar general of the diocese, and in 1930 he was sent to be the cathedral administrator. He was appointed as a domestic prelate to Pope Pius XI—i.e. a monsignor. In 1934, he was appointed canon theologian to the cathedral chapter. He was well-known around Newcastle and took a great interest in the parish schools, encouraging their development and growth.

Following the death of Bishop Thorman, McCormack was elected vicar capitular by the chapter, that is, he was given the responsibility of the diocese during the *sede vacante* between the death of one bishop and the installation of the next. Following this period, McCormack was appointed Bishop of Hexham and Newcastle on 30 December 1936 by Pope Pius XI. He was ordained bishop in St Mary's Cathedral on 4 February 1937 by Archbishop Richard Downey (Liverpool), assisted by Bishop Thomas Shine (Middlesbrough) and Bishop John Poskitt (Leeds). The day chosen for the ordination was significant: the diocesan feast day commemorating Blessed John Speed and his companions, who were hanged in Durham in 1594.

The *Catholic Herald* reported impressive scenes in Newcastle. The cathedral was filled to capacity, with over 270 priests present, and a vast crowd stood outside. Draped in papal colours (yellow and white), the "cathedral ... presented a scene of solemn splendour as the procession entered. Then the archbishop proceeded to the altar where he sat on the faldstool with his back to the altar and heard Mgr Adamson read the apostolic mandate authorizing the consecration."[3] Bishop McCormack was invested with St Cuthbert's episcopal ring, taken from the saint's finger when his tomb was opened in 1537. The ring is over 1300 years old but is thought to have been added to St Cuthbert's finger following his demise. "An address from the clergy of the diocese was read to the Bishop by the Provost of the Cathedral Chapter (Provost Henry Mackin)."[4]

Just a few months later (August 1937), the new bishop celebrated the silver jubilee of his priestly ordination, offering a Solemn High Mass of Thanksgiving in the cathedral church. The church was again crowded with priests and laity from all parts of the diocese.

In September 1939, England entered the Second World War. Much of the diocese being very rural, it became a safe haven for evacuees and refugees. In 1939, the bishop wrote in his Advent pastoral letter:

> The Armed forces and evacuees—our first duty must be to provide for our forces who daily have to face death—they must have priests to give what only a priest can give: Mass Communion, Absolution. The evacuated children must be catered for, I owe this to their dear parents who look to me with confidence. Many have turned to God in this dark hour. It is not unusual to find 400 at night prayers in our larger parishes and sometimes 600 at Morning Mass.[5]

But, of course, a significant part of the diocese was not rural, indeed it was highly industrialized, and, as part of Hitler's "War Directive no. 9", the North-East, particularly its steelworks, shipbuilding yards, docks and transport infrastructure, was considered an important target. The first air raid on Newcastle and Gateshead occurred on the afternoon of 2 July 1940. The target was the High Level Bridge. Thirteen people were killed and 231 injured. Further evacuations of schoolchildren took place, and on 18 July high explosive bombs were dropped again, killing three and severely damaging Heaton Secondary School.

The next large-scale raid took place on 15 August, and although British fighters intercepted much of the incoming force and brought down seventy-five enemy bombers, bombs were dropped on Newcastle and Sunderland. Air raids continued in the Heaton area in September. In April 1941, there was another concerted attack, causing many fires: homes were damaged as well as Cambridge Street School and St Michael's RC Church. Later in the month a shower of incendiary bombs fell in the South Shields area, killing forty-seven people and injuring seventy. Homes and shops were damaged. Further raids took place in September and December 1941. When New Bridge Street Goods Station was bombed, it burned for a week. Over a thousand people were made homeless. A number of churches were seriously damaged by enemy action, including St Cuthbert's North Shields, St Cecilia's Sunderland, St Mary's Sunderland and, as already mentioned, St Michael's in Newcastle.

Possibly as an acknowledgement of the particularly severe attacks on the North-East, on 18 June 1941 the King and Queen went to Tyneside and visited shipyards and armament factories, and again in April 1943. In July 1941, the Princess Royal visited the HQ of the Northumberland

and Durham War Needs Fund, and in November 1941, Prime Minister Winston Churchill paid a surprise visit to Tyneside.

The bishop had to contend with bombing damage to diocesan churches and buildings, while his own house, the Bishop's House in Front Street, Tynemouth, was damaged too. In 1941, the church and the presbytery there (which was the Bishop's House) were damaged by the explosion in the castle ditch of a sea-mine intended for the harbour. The doors and windows of the church were blown out, and the roof was badly damaged too. The presbytery next door was also so badly damaged that the bishop could no longer live there.[6]

He lodged in temporary accommodation for a brief while but then moved, in 1942, to a new bishop's house at 800 West Road, East Denton, just over three miles from Newcastle city centre. East Denton Hall was built by Anthony Errington and dates from 1622. It is a substantial sandstone, three-storeyed property with a Welsh slate roof, set in just over five acres. In the eighteenth century, the hall was the seat of the prominent Montague family and was also for a time a convent, so was suitably equipped with a chapel. This would be the home of all the bishops of Hexham and Newcastle until 2020, when Bishop Byrne moved residence again.

On 8 May 1945, the end of the European war was declared and a proclamation was read by the Lord Mayor in St Nicholas' Square, followed by the lighting of celebratory bonfires and, once again, the floodlighting of major buildings. A victory parade took place on 13 May. But, of course, the hard work of rebuilding then had to begin. A huge secular house-building project was undertaken, and Bishop McCormack was engaged in a similarly mammoth task of rebuilding parishes and establishing new ones too. For example, the roof of St Mary's Sunderland had to be rebuilt, and the stained glass which had all been destroyed was replaced in 1946 and 1947. The new glass cost £1,000 and came from Jansens and Company, a Dutch glassmaker. Similarly, the altars and the Stations of the Cross were repaired. When all was complete, Bishop McCormack consecrated the church on 24 September 1947.

In 1949, Bishop McCormack consecrated the church of St Bede in South Shields. Originally, the Catholics of South Shields would have had to cross the Tyne, by boat, to go to Mass at St Cuthbert's in North Shields.

On 4 December 1849, Bishop Hogarth opened the first Catholic church in South Shields, in the former chapel of the Bristol Brethren, located in St Cuthbert Street, now the Western Approach. By 1870, the community had outgrown this little chapel, and Canon Waterton acquired a site in Westoe Road upon which to build a new church to designs by Thomas C. Nicholson, in the Early English Gothic style. The foundation stone was laid on 27 May 1874, and the church opened on 22 August 1876, but there were problems with quicksand and subsidence, and deeper foundations had to be dug. The costs soared from an estimated £8,000 to £11,000 and the building of the north-west tower had to be abandoned. Some of the stained glass from the original chapel was moved to the new church. Despite a variety of benefactions, the debts of course were considerable, so it was not until 14 September 1949 that St Bede's, South Shields was finally consecrated by Bishop McCormack. The church was refurbished in 1965 and re-ordered in 1972, following the reforms of the Second Vatican Council.

I have already mentioned St Patrick's, Felling, a number of times in this text. Bishop Wilkinson opened the church in 1895, and Bishop Thorman laid the foundation stone for the new (St Alban's) school in 1927. What is not always realized is that a church cannot be consecrated until all its debts have been paid off, and this is often some time after the original opening. The consecration of St Patrick's Church fell to Bishop McCormack on 24 May 1950. The church was filled to capacity, and eight Felling-born priests, as well as a number of other clergy, took part in a ceremony which lasted nearly four hours. The bishop sprinkled the walls inside and out with holy water. He anointed the twelve marble crosses on the walls, consecrated the main altar and installed the relics while the cantors and choir sang appropriate psalms and canticles.

In what is perhaps the most theatrical part of the consecration ceremony,

> the bishop traced with his crozier the letters of the Greek and Latin alphabets in little heaps of ashes which had been sprinkled on the floor of the church. In two lines—one of 24 heaps for the Greek alphabet, and the other of 23 for the Latin—they took the shape of a Greek cross. This symbolized the two languages of

the church—Greek in the past and Latin at the present time—by which the people came to the knowledge of Christianity.[7]

I have mentioned above that, as vicar general, McCormack was particularly involved with the Catholic schools in the diocese. Following the passing of the 1944 Education Act, McCormack became significantly involved with education again, only this time at an episcopal level. The 1944 Act, known as the Butler Act after R. A. Butler, was far-reaching, but the three principal changes were first to create a Ministry of Education, under a secretary of state who had a seat in the cabinet. This ministry replaced the former School Boards. Secondly, the Act raised the school leaving age to fifteen (from 1947) with the intention that it be raised to sixteen as soon as this became practicable. And thirdly, the Act abolished all-age elementary schools and legislated for local authorities to provide three stages of education: primary, secondary and further.

The part of the Act that was significant for Catholics was the new provision for church schools. Although not immediately implemented, the future structure was enshrined in law. There were essentially two options. Voluntary Controlled (VC) schools were entirely state-funded; a foundation or trust (usually a Christian denomination) had some limited influence on the running of the school, but it would be ultimately controlled by the Local Education Authority. A Voluntary Aided (VA) school would have its running costs met by the state, but a foundation or trust would own or part-own the fabric and buildings of the school and would then have a substantial influence on the running of the school with mandatory representation on the board of governors.

Although many Church of England schools became VC schools, Catholics were concerned that in such schools a distinctly Catholic ethos would be lost, a Catholic curriculum (especially in religious education) would be diluted, and there might be insufficient Catholic staff, particularly at a leadership level. On the other hand, they argued that to adopt the VA model, retaining the possibility of Catholic education for Catholic children, would mean that Catholic children were provided with less state funding than their counterparts not in VA schools, and this was argued to be unfair. Furthermore, on a practical level, funds would need to be found for the financing of Catholic VA schools.

The situation rather came to a head in 1948, when the Ministry of Education required schools applying for VA status to demonstrate that they were ready and able to meet their share of the costs, in particular the costs of altering, repairing and equipping schools, especially in the light of new building regulations and the rapidly increasing child population after the war. The Catholic hierarchy, seeking to provide a Catholic education for every Catholic child, sought various amendments and an understanding interpretation of the legislation, while some in government were opposed to any special measures for Catholics. Here is not the place to enter into the details of this debate, save to say, firstly, that it was not really until the energetic Bishop Beck (1904–78) was appointed to be chairman of the Catholic Education Council, in 1949, that something of a crusade for Catholic education began.

And secondly, Bishop McCormack in the North-East was very much a part of this crusade. Bishop Beck organized a series of rallies to promote Catholic education, and McCormack spoke at the second of these, warning of the grave dangers to Catholic schools. Under the headline "No Protestant Syllabus", the *Catholic Herald* reported:

> Last Sunday more than 3,000 Tyneside people attended a mass meeting of the Newcastle Catholic Schools Committee in the City Hall and another 800 filled the overflow meeting in the Baths Hall. Almost 1,000 more people were unable to gain admittance to either meeting. Mgr Joseph McCormack, Bishop of Hexham and Newcastle, was the principal speaker.... The Bishop summed up the position of Catholic schools under the terms of the White Paper and reading excerpts from the letter of Mr Butler published last week, said that there was hope that better terms may yet be offered.[8]

This pressure prompted Winston Churchill to declare that it was "no part of Conservative policy to administer denominational schools out of existence".[9] At one point, McCormack proposed that the denominational VA schools should have financial responsibility for the classrooms only, leaving the remainder to the local authority. This clever ruse was supported by the Church of England, and this regrettably led to it being unsuccessful, as the C of E had, in the main, accepted the principle of VC schools, and the diminishing involvement of the churches in education.

McCormack made no such concessions and maintained that Catholics should be afforded the liberty of conscience so that Catholic children could be taught the Catholic faith, by Catholic teachers in a Catholic atmosphere. Further, he maintained that in some dioceses, and surely he was thinking of his own among others, the financial burden that Catholics were being asked to bear was, in addition to their rates and taxes which were to pay for education, unacceptable. If Bishops Chadwick and Bewick were champions of Catholic education in the North-East in the nineteenth century, then McCormack was certainly their successor in the twentieth.

On 12 March 1951, McCormack, along with Bishop John Petit (Menevia), assisted Archbishop Godfrey at the episcopal ordination of Bishop (later Cardinal) John Heenan, who would later preach at McCormack's funeral. Heenan recalls an amusing misunderstanding:

> There was a hitch at the start which led to a long and baffling delay while the congregation became increasingly restive. I was dressed in purple for the first time. I felt young, thin and frail. I had a headache of such severity that I could scarcely read the print in the missal. I was led by my assistants, Bishop McCormack and Bishop Petit, to a side altar to vest while the chief-consecrator, the Apostolic Delegate, was vesting at the high altar. Unfortunately the side altar was out of sight of the high altar. For nearly a quarter of an hour the master of ceremonies waited for my procession to emerge from the side chapel while we were waiting for a signal to proceed![10]

In 1956, McCormack founded the *Northern Cross* newspaper, a monthly publication for the Christian community in North-East England, particularly the diocese of Hexham and Newcastle. The first issue appeared in January 1956, and it is still published on the first Sunday of every month. The newspaper aims to enhance and promote a greater understanding of Christianity, to support and encourage the faithful, and to encourage greater participation in parish life and within the

Catholic community and other Christian churches locally, nationally and internationally. The newspaper received a papal blessing on 11 September 1965.

Bishop McCormack died at Bishop's House, 800 West Road, Newcastle on 2 March 1958 (aged seventy). His funeral and Pontifical Requiem Mass were celebrated in St Mary's Cathedral, where four archbishops (including the Apostolic Delegate Archbishop O'Hara), eleven bishops and some 400 clergy joined together. Archbishop Heenan, who preached the homily, spoke of a beloved bishop whose task was done. He went on to say:

> It would be easy to give you a long list of his virtues. His affection for his priests, his love for his flock especially for his children were well-known. His pastoral zeal, inherited from outstanding apostolic bishops, enabled him to continue traditions which have made this diocese of Hexham and Newcastle a model to the country and to the Catholic world.[11]

After the Mass, Bishop McCormack's cortège passed through streets lined with hundreds of people to Ushaw, where his body was interred at the cemetery there.

Notes

1. *Catholic Herald*, 7 March 1958.
2. C. Hart, *The Early Story of St Cuthbert's Grammar School* (London: Burns & Oates, 1941), p. 127.
3. *Catholic Herald*, 12 February 1937.
4. Ibid.
5. Advent pastoral letter 1939, quoted in Brian Plumb, *Arundel to Zabi: A Biographical Dictionary of the Catholic Bishops of England and Wales (Deceased) 1623–2000* (Wigan: North West Catholic History Society, 1987, 2006), p. 141.
6. See Fr A. Pickering, *Our Lady and St Oswin, Tynemouth and Cullercoats: Story of our Parish* (Tynemouth, 1990), pp. 11–12.
7. Tom R. Sterling, *St Patrick's RC Church, Felling, 1895–2014* (2014), <http://www.stpatricks-felling.co.uk/wp-content/uploads/The-history-of-St-Patricks-Booklet-1.pdf>, accessed 2 November 2021, p. 72.
8. *Catholic Herald*, 1 October 1943.
9. F. Phillips, *Bishop Beck and English Education, 1949–1959* (Lampeter: Edward Mellin Press, 1990), p. 24.
10. John Heenan, *A Crown of Thorns* (London: Hodder and Stoughton, 1974), p. 19.
11. See *Catholic Herald*, 14 March 1958.

9

James Cunningham (1958–74)

James Cunningham was born on 15 August 1910 at Heald Grove, Rusholme, Manchester. His father was Patrick Cunningham, originally from Sligo in Ireland, and his mother was Elizabeth née Maye. The family owned and ran a laundry business in Nelson Street in Rusholme.

Cunningham was educated at St Edward's Catholic Elementary School and as a boy would often serve the Mass at nearby St Edward's Church. It is said to be this that set him thinking about becoming a priest. His secondary education was at the Xaverian College, then a grammar school, in Manchester. He then went to St Joseph's College, Upholland, to study for the priesthood. Regrettably no more, having closed in 1987, Upholland was founded in 1880 by Bishop Bernard O'Reilly to be a seminary for North-West England, and in particular for the diocese of Liverpool. The college was "an ample and in parts handsome, sandstone building in wide grounds with two lakes and an extensive farm and orchards".[1] At its height, there was a junior seminary for schoolboys and a major seminary preparing men for ordination: some 200 boys and men in total.

Sir Anthony Kenny, who was a pupil at the junior seminary there some twenty years after Cunningham, gives us something of the liturgical flavour as he recalls:

> the offices of Holy Week and of Christmas were the climax of the year at Upholland. The Christmas Office lasted from 10pm on Christmas Eve until about 2am: first the Christmas Matins (nine psalms, lessons and antiphons), then the Midnight Mass, and immediately afterwards the Christmas Lauds (five psalms, a hymn and a canticle). . . . But for overall dramatic effect the

Christmas Office was far outdone by the ceremonies of Holy Week. The entire week before Easter Sunday was given over to religious observances.²

A retreat took place in the first part of Holy Week. The elaborate services of the triduum were performed with great precision following careful rehearsal.

Cunningham was ordained to the priesthood at Upholland, for the diocese of Salford, on 22 May 1937, by Bishop Thomas Henshaw (1873–1938). Following his ordination, he was sent to the Beda College in Rome for three years, where he studied canon law at the Gregorian University, which awarded his Licence in Canon Law or JCL.

In 1949, Cunningham returned to the diocese of Salford and was appointed assistant priest at the cathedral. The following year he was also appointed as secretary to Bishop Henry Marshall, a post which he held for twelve years. In 1953, Cunningham was appointed administrator of Salford Cathedral, vicar general and a domestic prelate—a monsignor. The following year he was appointed as a canon of the Salford Cathedral chapter. On the death of Bishop Marshall (14 April 1955), Cunningham was appointed vicar capitular, effectively ruling Salford diocese, until Bishop Beck was appointed later that same year.

In August 1957, Cunningham was appointed Titular Bishop of Jos and Auxiliary Bishop of Hexham and Newcastle, by Pope Pius XII. On 12 November, he was ordained bishop in St Mary's Cathedral, Newcastle, by the Archbishop of Liverpool, John Heenan, assisted by Bishop George Beck (Salford) and Bishop George Brunner (Middlesbrough). The cathedral was filled to capacity and many more people gathered outside. Bishop McCormack was unable to be present on account of his health, but Cunningham's brother attended with his wife. Following the Mass, there was a reception for civic leaders at La Sagesse Convent and a reception for the faithful of the diocese at Sacred Heart College, Fenham.³

Less than a year later, Bishop McCormack died and Cunningham served as vicar capitular, very unusually for the second time, until he was appointed Bishop of Hexham and Newcastle. Fr Edward Harriott of St Andrew's Newcastle observed:

> As Vicar general under bishop Beck he so endeared himself to the clergy and people of the Salford Diocese that his promotion to Auxiliary Bishop of Hexham and Newcastle on 24 August 1957, was felt by them to be great personal loss. But their loss is our gain. During the four months that have elapsed since the sad decease of Bishop McCormack, he has already given evidence as Vicar Capitular, of his organizing ability, his wide interests and his untiring zeal.[4]

It is not certain that Cunningham really wanted to leave his native Salford, but he was made welcome in the North-East and soon settled. It was the first time since Bishop O'Callaghan's appointment in 1887 that an appointment was made from outside the diocese.

He was enthroned in the cathedral on Wednesday 30 October by Archbishop Heenan, who celebrated a Pontifical High Mass, and Bishop Beck preached the homily. He was given the episcopal ring of St Cuthbert and a new crozier, a gift from the people of Hexham and Newcastle.

Bishop Cunningham's arrival coincided with the centenary celebration of the Marian apparitions in Lourdes in 1858. In the diocese, "there was a mime written by Hugh Ross Williamson, a cantata composed by Edmund Rubbra, sermons by the future Cardinal Gray and numerous processions of 10,000 participants accompanied by the colliery bands of Hylton, Ryhope and Esh."[5]

In 1962, Bishop Cunningham was appointed to be a Father at the Second Vatican Council, all four sessions of which he attended. Angelo Giuseppe Roncalli (1881-1963) was elected to the papacy as Pope John XXIII, on 18 October 1958, and in the following January he announced his intention to convoke an Ecumenical Council. He wrote in his *Journal of a Soul*: "O Divine Spirit, sent by the Father in the name of Jesus, give your aid and infallible guidance to your Church and pour out on the Ecumenical Council the fullness of your gifts. O gentle Teacher and Consoler, enlighten the hearts of our prelates who, eagerly responding to the call of the Supreme Roman Pontiff, will gather here in solemn conclave."[6] At this stage it was, in fact, just an announcement of the Pope's intention to call a council and the formal summons was not made until *Humanae salutis* was promulgated on 25 December 1961.

Unlike many of the previous councils, this was not designed to clarify or update Church doctrine but was famously convened in a spirit of *aggiornamento*—to open the windows (of the Church) and let in some fresh air. The aim of the Council was to bring the Church up to date: to review its relationship with, and mission to, the world. More recently Pope Benedict XVI has affirmed that the most important message of the Council is "the Paschal mystery at the centre of what it is to be Christian and therefore of the Christian life, the Christian year, the Christian seasons".[7]

The Council was formally opened on 11 October 1962 and had eleven commissions and three secretariats which would finally produce four constitutions, three declarations and nine decrees, although here is not the place to review all the work of the Council.

Back from Rome, a new sense of ecumenism was in the air and a reception was held to which other Christians and representatives of the Jewish community were invited. It sounds commonplace to modern ears, but at the time marked a significant departure from what had gone before and laid the foundations of future ecumenical and inter-faith relationships which are a notable feature of religious life in the North-East.

Cunningham was also involved, at least peripherally, with the work of ICEL. The International Commission on English in the Liturgy was established in 1963 during the Second Vatican Council by episcopal conferences from anglophone countries to provide English translations of the (Latin) liturgical books of the Roman Rite. In the late 1960s, Canon John McHugh (1927–2006), a theologian at Ushaw and later Durham University, prepared translations of Vespers and Compline for use at Ushaw, sending these as proposals for the new English Breviary to Bishop Cunningham. McHugh also prepared translations of various collects, Eucharistic Prayers II and III, and a notably fine English version of the *Exsultet*. The translations were not supposed to be literal translations but what came to be called "dynamic equivalences" capturing the meaning of the prayers. Such translations are inevitably controversial, and it is noteworthy that, through collaboration with McHugh, Bishop Cunningham would have had an indirect involvement with liturgical translations and the work of ICEL.

Also, Cunningham was involved in, and indeed managed and guided, local post-Conciliar changes, and this proved to be another period of considerable growth in the diocese. During Cunningham's episcopate, some fifty churches and eighty schools were built, and the Catholic population of the diocese rose by ten percent to 275,000.

For example, one of these churches was the new church of St Cuthbert's at Seaham, near Sunderland, which Cunningham opened in 1965. The people there had worshipped in a temporary chapel for thirty-two years! The new building, to a design by David Brown, was a modern interpretation of the Gothic style, with notable stained glass by Maralyn O'Keefe. Fr John Gits was appointed to the parish in 1934 and died just before the new church was completed. The interior of the church was re-ordered in 1991.

By 1974, Bishop Cunningham's health had begun to decline, and he resigned his see on 16 May on the grounds of ill-health, and his resignation was accepted by Pope Paul VI.[8] Less than two months later he died, in the General Hospital in Newcastle, on 10 July 1974, aged sixty-three. After his Requiem Mass, his body was buried at Ushaw. The memorial plaque in the cloisters there describes him as a "simple, upright and God-fearing man" (*Vir simplex et rectus ac timens Deum*).

Notes

1. Anthony Kenny, *A Path from Rome* (London: Sidgwick and Jackson, 1985), p. 23.
2. Ibid., p. 31.
3. See *Catholic Herald*, 15 November 1957.
4. *Catholic Herald*, 11 July 1958.
5. Brian Plumb, *Arundel to Zabi: A Biographical Dictionary of the Catholic Bishops of England and Wales (Deceased) 1623–2000* (Wigan: North West Catholic History Society, 1987, 2006), p. 76.
6. Pope John XXIII, *Journal of a Soul*, tr. Dorothy White (London: Geoffrey Chapman, 1965), p. 391 (23 September 1959).
7. Meeting with the Parish Priests and Clergy of Rome Diocese, 14 February 2013.
8. See *Catholic Herald*, 24 May 1974.

1 0

Hugh Lindsay (1974-92)

Hugh Lindsay succeeded Bishop James Cunningham as the tenth Bishop of Hexham and Newcastle. He was born on 20 June 1927 in Jesmond in Newcastle upon Tyne. He was one of five children and the son of William Lindsay, a draper, and his wife Mary. There is a story that, when he was only four years old, an older girl pointed to a priest smoking a pipe, telling him that she could see his future there. He replied, he wouldn't smoke a pipe!

He went to school at St Charles, Gosforth, from 1932 and then to St Andrew's, Newcastle from 1936. In 1938, he went up to St Cuthbert's Grammar School, which opened in 1881, largely due to the efforts of Bishop Chadwick and his successor Bishop Bewick. The school was originally located in Eldon Square and subsequently moved to Bath Lane, then Benwell Hill. Lindsay was there for just a year until he, and the whole school, were evacuated to Cockermouth until 1941. During the war years, his parents' drapery shop suffered from the effects of the Depression, and the family struggled to make ends meet. This gave him an insight, at first hand, into poverty and the fragility of the economy in the North-East.

The effects of evacuation would have left their mark too. At 11 a.m. on 31 August 1939, the Ministry of Health gave the order to evacuate forthwith. The following day children started to board trains moving from urban centres to the countryside. A total of 31,222 schoolchildren left Newcastle schools on 1 September, and a further 12,818 mothers and children under age left on 2 September. War was declared on 3 September. In total, an estimated 206,500 children were evacuated from Newcastle, Gateshead, Tynemouth, Wallsend and North and South Shields.[1] They were sent to rural areas of Northumberland and Durham, but also Cumberland, as in the case of the St Cuthbert's boys, Lancashire and even America and Australia. By early 1940, the bombing had not really begun, and some 40 per cent of children had returned home, but, as is well known, the timescale of the war was badly underestimated.

In 1943, Lindsay was accepted as a candidate for the priesthood and went to study at Ushaw College. In September 1945, his studies were interrupted when he was called up for military service, although seminarians were exempt. Lindsay saw this service as a civil duty, and he joined the RAF. He completed basic training and then in 1946 was posted to India, where he served in Madras, primarily in an administrative role, and then at the Air Headquarters in New Delhi until January 1948. Thereafter, he returned to his studies at Ushaw and was ordained priest at the hands of Bishop McCormack in St Mary's Cathedral, for the diocese of Hexham and Newcastle, on 19 July 1953.

His first appointment was to the Church of St Lawrence in Byker, a working-class area of Newcastle, and the following year (1954) he went on to St Matthew's, Ponteland. During this time, he also assisted at Bishop's House as diocesan secretary, where his diligence and administrative know-how were put to good use.

In March 1959, he was appointed bishop's secretary to Bishop James Cunningham, a post he held for ten years. By some accounts Bishop Cunningham was typical of the bishops of his era, remote and authoritative, but the two men got on well.[2] The story is told that when, on one occasion, Fr Lindsay was assisting Bishop Cunningham at Mass, the bishop realized that he was missing a book containing a particular prayer. He sent Lindsay off to the sacristy to fetch the book, but when he returned, he discovered that Bishop Cunningham had recited the prayer by heart!

Owing to Bishop Cunningham's declining health, Pope Paul VI appointed Lindsay auxiliary bishop on 13 October 1969. When the apostolic delegate summoned him to announce the appointment, he told Lindsay, in Latin, that he would be the Titular Bishop of Cuncacestre. Lindsay recalled thinking, "Where the hell's that?" The delegate, sensing his puzzlement, told him—Chester-le-Street—halfway between Durham and Newcastle and an ancient Saxon see.

On 11 December, he was ordained Titular Bishop of Cuncacestre and Auxiliary Bishop of Hexham and Newcastle, by Archbishop Andrew

Beck (Liverpool) assisted by Bishops John McClean (Middlesbrough) and James Hagan (Titular Bishop of Horrea Coelia). Aged forty-two, he was, at the time, the youngest bishop in the English hierarchy.

Bishop Cunningham resigned from Hexham and Newcastle on 16 May 1974 and died on 10 July the same year, and was succeeded by Lindsay, who was installed on 12 December 1974. As a bishop, Lindsay adopted a distinctly collaborative approach to leadership, discussing matters with both clergy and laity and aiming for a consensus. He was in sympathy with the reforms of the Second Vatican Council, but his critics accused him of being slow to implement them, on account of his preference for consultation. In general, he recognized a diversity of opinions, but he was not a traditionalist. Having said that, he was not a liberal either, and when vandals broke into a church in Jarrow in the 1970s and desecrated the tabernacle, scattering the communion hosts, he ordered all-night exposition of the Blessed Sacrament in all churches throughout the diocese in reparation for the sacrilege.

Lindsay was not in favour of the celebration of the old, or "Tridentine", rite of the Mass, although a number of his fellow bishops were more ambivalent. Archbishop Heenan in Liverpool had voted against the introduction of the *Missa Normativa*, although loyally attempted to introduce it despite his better judgement. He instructed that at least one Sunday Mass each week should be in Latin, although according to the new form. Additionally, in October 1971, he petitioned the Pope to allow the occasional celebration of the old rite Mass according to the indult that existed. Bishop Bowen of Portsmouth, and subsequently Archbishop of Southwark, is also noted for his sympathy towards the old rite of the Mass.

Looking back to the early 1970s, it is easy to see that, beyond personal preference, there were bishops who wanted to embrace the vision of the Council and abolish all the old ways. And there were those bishops who wanted to emphasize the continuity between the pre- and post-Conciliar Church. Of course, some of those in favour of the old rite were also suspected to be in sympathy with the schismatic Archbishop Marcel Lefebvre, and to this day liturgical arguments cannot be dissociated from wider theological disagreements.

In other ways, Bishop Lindsay was quite forward-looking and is said to have been one of the very first church leaders to have a computer terminal on his desk, and for this he was featured in the business pages of *The Sunday Times* in the 1980s. No doubt this enabled him to pen many letters, and he was well-known as a keen contributor to the letters pages of Catholic journals, where he refuted error and misunderstanding.

He was an active and busy member of the Bishops' Conference. He was a member of the Laity Commission and the Mass Media Commission, and he chaired the Catholic Information Office, now renamed the News and Media Department. This important department releases news, statements and comments from the bishops to the press and other agencies.

Lindsay was also involved in a working party on pastoral strategy which sought to update the Church's position and produced the forward-looking report "Church 2000". Michael Winter in the *Catholic Herald* of 29 June 1973 praised the "beautiful ideas" in the report, which called for smaller dioceses, better training of priests, more effective roles for the laity etc. Nevertheless, he expressed some disappointment that there was little detail on how these laudable aims would be achieved. In fairness, the document was envisaged as a starting point for dialogue, but Winter complained that a proper method and suitable terms of reference were not clearly articulated.

Having said this, Lindsay kept a naturally low profile, seeing the bishop's office as one of service rather than personal honour. He identified strongly with the local area and worked strenuously to promote the welfare of his people, raising his voice against poverty and unemployment on a number of occasions.

It was while Lindsay was Bishop of Hexham and Newcastle that Pope (now St) John Paul II made his historic visit to Britain in May 1982. In the end, the visit was a great success, but at one point it was nearly cancelled since the United Kingdom, at that time, was in conflict with Argentina over the Falkland Islands. Following a frantic diplomatic effort, compromise was reached, whereby Pope John Paul II visited both the UK and Argentina. The high point of the UK trip was perhaps the service in Canterbury Cathedral jointly presided over by the Pope and Archbishop Runcie, and the subsequent signing of a Common Declaration of Unity.

The theme of the Pope's six-day visit was the seven sacraments, an idea proposed by Michael Bowen, Archbishop of Southwark. One of the most memorable images of the visit was the day when the Pope visited

St George's Cathedral in Southwark, which had been transformed into a giant hospital ward for the day, to celebrate the sacrament of the sick and a Mass for the sick. The day itself was "a moment of great joy for the archbishop, and was always recalled by the Pope whenever the two met in Rome".[3]

A number of amusing incidents were connected with the visit. The first was that, as Gatwick lay in the diocese of Arundel and Brighton, Bishop Cormac Murphy-O'Connor was detailed to make the formal welcome. There was something of a mix-up and the minibus due to take the Pope and his entourage to the station for the papal train took them to the terminal building instead, and they missed the train. Three cars and six police outriders were summoned for the top-speed, forty-five-minute drive to Westminster Cathedral. With no little irony, the late Mgr Richard Stewart recalled the opening words of the Pope at the cathedral: "With heartfelt gratitude and love I thank our Lord and Saviour Jesus Christ that he has given me the grace of coming among you today."[4]

Murphy-O'Connor also tells the amusing story that when they were in Glasgow the crowds sang "Will ye no come back again?", and the Pope turned to Archbishop Thomas Winning, the Archbishop of Glasgow, and asked him what the words of the song they kept repeating meant. Tom explained that the song referred to Bonnie Prince Charlie. "Oh I know him," the Pope replied, "I met him in Canterbury last week!"[5]

In 1987, Lindsay's health began to deteriorate: he had back problems which caused him acute discomfort, and he had to have two surgical operations on his back. By 1992, he felt he no longer had the strength to carry out his duties, and he offered his resignation, which was reluctantly accepted by Pope John Paul II on 11 January 1992. He moved to the diocese of Lancaster, to Boarbank Hall, Grange-over-Sands in Cumbria, where he acted as chaplain to a community of Augustinian Canonesses. He lived with the Sisters for the remainder of his life and was cared for by them.

While at Boarbank, he continued a very regular correspondence to the press, writing to national newspapers whenever he felt the Church was being unfairly portrayed. He called for accuracy and fair play, countered misunderstandings and explained Church teaching. For example, when Ruth Gledhill wrote in *The Times* that "for decades bishops and priests in the Church were forced to obey a policy of absolute secrecy on the subject of sexual abuse by priests on pain of expulsion",[6] Lindsay wrote forcefully that there was no such policy. Recalling his ten years as a bishop's secretary and his own eighteen years as a bishop, he wrote: "No one has mentioned either the document or the policy to me: moreover I was never asked about it in my frequent report to the Vatican or during my visits to the Roman Curia."[7] Of course this does not prove the point and a cynic might say that "he would say that, wouldn't he?", but such an attitude is more conspiracy theory than balanced judgement.

Bishop Lindsay died on 19 January 2009. He was said to be frail but fit for his age. His Requiem Mass and funeral took place in Newcastle Cathedral, on 2 February, presided over by Bishop Ambrose Griffiths. Fr John Butters preached the homily, remarking that it was in the cathedral that Lindsay had been baptized almost eighty-two years previously. Butters described Lindsay as a good and decent man who explained and defended the gospel and the Catholic faith. His remarks provoked laughter when he recalled that Bishop Lindsay would often begin by saying that he had three things to say—but that number could be doubled at the drop of a mitre! Severe weather conditions on the day prevented a number of people, including Cardinal Murphy-O'Connor, from attending.

After the Requiem, Bishop Lindsay was buried in the cathedral crypt. A notice outside the cathedral reads:

> This memorial (possibly designed by the cathedral architect A W N Pugin) marks the position of a vaulted crypt below, containing the bodies of Bishop William Riddell (d. 1847) and Father William Fletcher (d. 1848), both victims of a typhus epidemic. The inscription begins Sub hoc lapide iacet corpus Gulielmi Riddell Episcopi, qui hanc ecclesiam fieri fecit . . . (Under this stone lies the body of Bishop William Riddell who caused this church to be built . . .). The crypt remained sealed for many years until it was opened to receive the bodies of Bishop Kevin Dunn (d. 2008) and Bishop Hugh Lindsay (d. 2009).

Notes

1. Berwick Record Office (BRO): 794/62/5, "Government Evacuation Scheme", Ministry of Health Circular 37/5.
2. See *The Times*, 20 January 2009.
3. Quoted in Bowen's obituary in *The Tablet*, 31 October 2019.
4. John Stapleton (ed.), *The A&B Story 1965-1990: The First Twenty Five Years* (The Diocese of Arundel and Brighton, 1990), p. 76.
5. Cormac Murphy-O'Connor, *An English Spring* (London: Bloomsbury, 2015), p. 124.
6. *The Times*, 18 August 2003.
7. Ibid., 20 August 2003.

10 A

Owen Francis Swindlehurst (1977–95)

In common with Bishop Preston, Bishop Swindlehurst is the only other auxiliary bishop of Hexham and Newcastle who was not translated to the diocesan see. He was born on 10 May 1928 at Newburn, in the Castle Ward, then in Northumberland. His father was Francis C. Swindlehurst, and his mother was Ellen née Woods. They were married in Durham in 1924. Owen had an elder brother, James, two years his senior.

Discerning an early vocation to the priesthood, he went to school at the junior seminary at Ushaw, where he flourished academically, and he was then sent (in 1948) to the Venerable English College in Rome, where, in due course, he became a senior student. He was awarded degrees in philosophy (PhL) and theology (STL), and later a doctorate in canon law (JCD), which he defended but did not publish. He was ordained priest, in Rome, for the diocese of Hexham and Newcastle, by Cardinal Traglia on 11 July 1954. Ten years in Rome left him with a lasting love of the place and all things Italian.

On his return to England, he undertook temporary appointments at St Matthew's, Jarrow, and St Joseph's, Blaydon, before his appointment as assistant priest at St Matthew's, Ponteland, from 1959, succeeding Fr Lindsay. He also worked as assistant diocesan secretary.

From Ponteland, he went (in April 1967) to St Bede's in Denton Burn near Newcastle and was then appointed parish priest of the Church of the Holy Name in Jesmond in February 1972, where he remained for ten years. He introduced the reforms of the Second Vatican Council, maintaining high liturgical standards and a weekly parish Mass with singing, helping those who felt sad at the loss of Latin.[1] He is also noted for his local ecumenical work, hosting a weekly prayer meeting with Anglican, Methodist and United Reformed Church clergy.

He was secretary to the diocesan council of priests, and in 1970 he was also appointed as the first diocesan representative to the newly formed National Conference of Priests. Although disbanded in 2010, for forty years this conference met annually at various venues to engage in ongoing formation and to participate in discussion and an exchange of views. The conference also acted as a national voice for English and Welsh priests. The records and minutes of the conferences are held in the Westminster diocesan archives.

Swindlehurst also served as Bishop Lindsay's secretary for ten years and was particularly involved in advising the bishop on canon law and assisting with marriage cases, in which he specialized. "He always balanced accurate legal knowledge with pastoral sensitivity. This was recognized by his fellow priests who regularly chose him to represent them at diocesan and national levels."[2] He is particularly remembered for his good judgement, keen sense of humour and the twinkle in his eye. In an oft-repeated story, Bishop Lindsay recalled that once when he had given a lengthy vote of thanks to a high official at the Roman Curia, Swindlehurst, who had been acting as his translator, said, with a glint in his eye, "*Sua Eccellenza è molto content*" (Bishop Lindsay is very grateful)!

Following Bishop Lindsay's installation as bishop there was widespread consultation about the appointment of an auxiliary, but it is said that it surprised nobody when, on 10 June 1977, Pope Paul VI appointed Swindlehurst Titular Bishop of Cuncacestre and Auxiliary Bishop of Hexham and Newcastle, with pastoral care for most of the Catholics between the Tyne and the Wear. He was ordained bishop in St Mary's Cathedral, Newcastle on 25 July 1977 by Bishop Hugh Lindsay, assisted by Cardinal Archbishop Basil Hume (Westminster) and Bishop Brian Foley (Lancaster). As bishop he took up residence with the Sisters of Mercy at Sunderland.

He is noted for his involvement in the Anglican/Roman Catholic joint school of St John and St Patrick in Sunderland, and he regularly visited diocesan schools. He is also remembered for his prison visits, and indeed it was his quiet care, often hidden from view, which was the hallmark of his ministry. Indeed, it is not for his legal or administrative skills that he is principally remembered, but as "an immensely successful pastoral bishop".[3]

Nevertheless, he was also noted for his expert knowledge on pro-life issues and sat on the Joint Bio-Ethical Committee alongside Scottish and Irish bishops. Later, at his death, Cardinal Basil Hume remarked that Swindlehurst had been his mother's parish priest (at Holy Name, Jesmond) in her later years and he also observed "It is not only the Diocese of Hexham and Newcastle which will be missing him but also our Bishops' Conference to which he made a considerable contribution, not only as a competent canon lawyer and theologian but also as a good friend to all his fellow bishops."[4]

When Bishop Lindsay was ill for several months in 1983, Swindlehurst ran the diocese and again much responsibility fell to him between 1989 and 1992. However, when Bishop Lindsay resigned on grounds of ill-health in February 1992, Swindlehurst was not appointed to succeed him but remained auxiliary under Bishop Griffiths, whom he co-consecrated. This is in no way a reflection on Swindlehurst's suitability for the post, save for his advancing years! He was sixty-four when Lindsay resigned, and his health was in decline too. As a younger man, he enjoyed long walks, particularly in his native Northumberland. He also played squash and was, incidentally, a devoted supporter of Newcastle United football team and a regular visitor to St James' Park. But these pastimes were gradually denied him.

Towards the end of his life, he succumbed to lung cancer, which took away his voice and his physical fitness. Despite this, he persevered with his treatment, including surgery, without complaint, speaking optimistically about the future right up to his last days. In this context, his friends and colleagues regarded his death, when it finally came, as a shock. He died in Sunderland on 28 August 1995 (aged sixty-seven).

His funeral, at which Bishop Lindsay preached, took place in the cathedral at Newcastle. The two men had worked closely together, both tall, quiet canon lawyers. Swindlehurst had succeeded Lindsay at Ponteland, as bishop's secretary and as auxiliary bishop. Both had suffered ill-health, and Lindsay said that he had expected to pre-decease Swindlehurst. Lindsay preached on the text "Happy the one who lives in the house of the Lord." Lindsay observed that this did not match his mood in the light of Bishop Owen's death, but that it captured Bishop Owen's life: "It was precisely for this happiness that Owen lived, worked, suffered and died."[5] Lindsay emphasized Swindlehurst's love of Italy and loyalty to Rome, but also to his family, his faith, the North-East and his diocese: low-key, incredibly talented and utterly dependable.

He is buried, along with his brother, in the churchyard of Our Lady Immaculate Catholic Church in Washington, County Durham. His tombstone reads:

> The Right Reverend Owen Francis Swindlehurst V.G. Bishop of Chester-Le-Street and Auxiliary of Hexham and Newcastle. Born 10th May 1928, Ordained Priest 11th July 1954, Ordained Bishop 25th July 1977, Died 28th August 1995. Faithful Pastor may you live with Christ. Requiescat in Pace.

Distasteful though it is, for the sake of completeness we should observe that, after his death, Bishop Swindlehurst was accused of the "cover-up" of priestly sexual abuse. Fr Adrian McLeish was jailed in 1996 after admitting twelve counts of abusing boys under fourteen and distributing child pornography. He alleged in a letter to a fellow priest that Bishop Swindlehurst knew of the abuse and even promoted him from assistant priest at Wallsend to parish priest at Gilesgate, in Durham, after which the abuse continued. Parents of the victims said the Church should have done more, and indeed the diocese made a payment of £10,000 damages but did not admit liability. Furthermore, the diocese insisted that there was no proof that Swindlehurst knew the details of the case.

Notes

[1] See obituary in *The Independent*, 10 September 1995.
[2] Ibid.
[3] Brian Plumb, *Arundel to Zabi: A Biographical Dictionary of the Catholic Bishops of England and Wales (Deceased) 1623–2000* (Wigan: North West Catholic History Society, 1987, 2006), p. 190.
[4] *Catholic Herald*, 1 September 1995.
[5] Bishop Lindsay's homily at Bishop Swindlehurst's Requiem, reproduced in *The Venerabile* XXXI:1 (1996), p. 54.

11

(John Michael Martin) Ambrose Griffiths (1992–2004)

Michael Griffiths was born in Twickenham on 4 December 1928 to parents Henry and Hilda Griffiths, who were both converts to Catholicism. The family was devout, and young Michael became involved in the local church from an early age. Michael had a brother three and a half years his senior: Anthony (later Canon) Griffiths. Young Michael went to a preparatory school in Brighton for a while before transferring to Ampleforth's own preparatory school: St Martin's, Gilling Castle. Thereafter he moved to Ampleforth College for his secondary education.

Following the Reformation, Dom Sigebert Buckley, the last monk of the community at Westminster (Abbey), joined monks of the English Cassinese Congregation and others, and established a Benedictine community at St Laurence, Dieulouard in France, in the first decade of the seventeenth century. For many years, monks were trained to work in the missions to England. The monks, like many other monks and nuns, were expelled from France at the Revolution and returned to England, finally settling at Ampleforth in 1802, and claiming a direct link to the ancient English congregation. The first abbey church was completed in 1857 but was demolished a century later to make way for a new church (dedicated to St Laurence the martyr), which had been begun in 1924 and was consecrated in 1961. The monks established a school, in 1803, which originally catered for seventy boys but in more recent times has grown almost tenfold and become co-educational.

Griffiths spent the war years at Ampleforth and excelled in his studies there, particularly in the sciences. His brother recalled that he was interested in science from an early age and that "when he was only about six or seven, my mother asked what he would like as a birthday treat. 'A whole day in the science museum,' he said. Sure enough, mother and he arrived almost as the doors opened. They were the last out as the doors closed. Michael was thrilled. My mother worn out."[1]

In 1946, when he was still only seventeen, Griffiths went up to Balliol College, Oxford (founded by John de Balliol in 1263) with a scholarship to study natural sciences, particularly chemistry. He was awarded a first-class bachelor's degree and subsequently MA (Oxon). In his first year, he shared a room at Balliol with a young Jewish student who subsequently converted to Catholicism, and thereafter he lodged at St Benet's Hall, the Ampleforth house for Benedictine students at Oxford. Upon completion of his studies at Oxford in 1950, it is said "he planned to become a research fellow in chemistry, but changed direction when a chemist in the college had a mental breakdown and destroyed all Griffiths' notes".[2]

Griffiths returned to Ampleforth and joined the religious community there, taking the name Ambrose, after the fourth-century Bishop of Milan. Writing of Basil Hume, also an Ampleforth monk, Michael Walsh has observed:

> Novices are not expected to enjoy the noviciate. It is a time of trials and petty humiliations designed to test the vocation, the determination and the endurance of the neophyte, cut off as novices are not just from their families but, rather oddly, from the community of monks which they are hoping to join.[3]

It is said that Basil Hume suffered from depression during his noviciate, and we may imagine that young brother Ambrose found it a challenging time too. Having said that, Griffiths' time at Ampleforth, and lodging at St Benet's Hall while in Oxford, would have prepared him to a certain extent and "his own youthful exuberance and easy sense of companionship ensured that he integrated well into community life ... [rather than] trying out a vocation ... in him [there was] a commitment that was already deeply formed".[4]

Griffiths was (simply) professed on 25 September 1951. Thereafter he was sent to the Anselmianum, the Pontifical Atheanaeum of St Anselm, in Rome, situated on the Aventine next door to the church of Sant'

Anselmo all'Aventino, to study theology. Founded by Pope Leo XIII in 1887, the Anselmianum is the Benedictine pontifical university in Rome, which provides theological training for Benedictines from around the world. Griffiths, by now Dom Ambrose (he was solemnly professed on 23 September 1954), was ordained priest, back in Ampleforth, on 21 July 1957.

Dom Ambrose's teaching career at Ampleforth extended from 1958 until 1972, and he taught science, RE and woodwork, eventually becoming head of science at the school. Basil Hume, five years older than him and ten years his senior in professed life, was head of modern languages. In later years, Griffiths, like Hume before him, was also engaged in teaching theology to the younger monks, particularly canon law and dogmatic theology:

> As a teacher of theology, he was both rigorous and open-minded, firmly grounded in the Thomistic tradition, but also alert to the new trains of thought that were being opened up at the time by the debates in the Second Vatican Council.[5]

In 1972, Griffiths was relieved of his teaching engagements and appointed procurator, or bursar, of the abbey, responsible for its day-to-day running and finances. The abbey site, which includes wooded areas, lakes and an apple orchard of some ten acres, as well as the school, the prep school and the abbey buildings themselves, is an enormous site (over 2,000 acres!) and Dom Ambrose would have been more than busy managing all the business and administrative aspects of monastery life. It is said that he had an eye for detail but also that he could engage with the "bigger picture". During his time as procurator, new classrooms, boarding houses and the St Alban (sports and swimming) Centre were built and, perhaps uniquely, under his leadership the first ever blueprint for future development was drawn up too.

He must have done a good job, for when Abbot Basil Hume was appointed Archbishop of Westminster in February 1976, the community elected Dom Ambrose to succeed him as the fifth Abbot of Ampleforth on 7 April. *The Rule of St Benedict* is clear: "The abbot is believed to act in the place of Christ in the monastery... and must show forth all good and holy things by his words and even more by his deeds."⁶ His abbatial style was a rare combination of organizational ability and efficiency tempered with patience and good humour. He was popular and respected, and he was kind, trusting and courteous to those in his care. Later, as a bishop, he would characterize his own position as holding fast to principles and always being patient and forgiving with people.

Abbot Ambrose was not re-elected at the elections of 1984. In an appreciation written by one of his fellow monks at the end of his abbacy, it was written that "few were more surprised than he was when we elected him, nobody was more grateful than he was when we elected another"! It is not uncommon for retired abbots to leave their monasteries, at least for a time, to allow the succeeding abbot a "free hand". Dom Ambrose was appointed to the honorary title of Abbot of Westminster and went to be parish priest of St Mary's, Leyland, in Lancashire. Benedictine priests went to Leyland in 1854 and have run the large and flourishing parish there, as an outpost of Ampleforth and with a Benedictine ethos, ever since. Griffiths would have been occupied with the day-to-day running of the parish and the usual round of services and other activities. It is said that he talked to everyone and threw himself into every aspect of parochial life from 6 a.m. to 11 p.m. He brought his wealth of experience in schools and of teaching to bear on the local Catholic schools, of which there were three in the parish. He united the parish about decisions that had to be made and ensured good governance throughout.

Nevertheless, "he was so shaken at first by the poverty in the area that he declined to take a holiday in the Holy Land when such a trip was clearly beyond the means of so many of his parishioners. Indeed he delighted in doing anything to help locals ..."⁷

In 1991, he reported back to the mother house at Ampleforth, writing:

> Our circular church is blessed with a wide ambulatory all round the church and a separate Blessed Sacrament chapel. This enabled us to hold not just a festival of flowers but also a festival of talents in which parishioners were encouraged to display things they had made. The results amazed every one and revealed an unexpected wealth of talent.

In a separate entry, he also wrote:

> Although the church is only twenty-five years old it has been necessary to replace the copper covering and underlay on the main roof and to rebuild the central lantern with new aluminium glazing bars. This has been completed during the last six months and the concrete bell tower has been renovated and treated to preserve it against the weather. The parish has responded splendidly to the problems and a third of the considerable cost has already been raised.[8]

In February 1992, Bishop Hugh Lindsay resigned as bishop on grounds of ill-health, and Pope (now St) John Paul II, having accepted Lindsay's resignation, announced Griffiths as his successor, the eleventh Bishop of Hexham and Newcastle. According to the story, Griffiths received a phone call from Liverpool asking him to visit the archbishop, who told him that the Pope had appointed him Bishop of Hexham and Newcastle. The following day, so surprised by the nomination, he telephoned "Archbishop Worlock in Liverpool to check that the offer was not just a dream. The efficient archbishop who had occasionally encountered vagueness amongst monks before, assured him that his memory was correct and the Pope did indeed want him to accept the appointment."[9] Moreover, it seemed that some senior English clerics (Derek Worlock, Basil Hume and Maurice Couve de Murville) pressed for his appointment too, fearful that Rome might appoint an Opus Dei priest or a conservative old Ushaw seminarian.[10]

Griffiths was ordained bishop on St Cuthbert's Day, 20 March 1992, by Archbishop Worlock, assisted by Bishop Hugh Lindsay (his predecessor) and Bishop Owen Swindlehurst (his auxiliary), and installed in the cathedral. The transition from monastery via parish to diocesan bishop was perhaps not always easy but Griffiths took it all in his stride. It is said that he arrived in the diocese like a gust of fresh air, well aware that the statistics suggested that the diocese might not exist by 2038 if the rate of decline continued. First he set up Bishop's House and invited three Sisters of Mercy from Oaklea Convent in Sunderland to become housekeepers.

Of course they had a job to do, but Griffiths also established something of the communal life that had nurtured him for so long.

Then he turned outwards and set himself to get to know the clergy and the laity of his new diocese. He travelled widely across the diocese, driving his own car, and would often "drop in" to visit his clergy if he was passing, sometimes, it is said, when a priest had already gone to bed! He made a special point of caring for his new clergy and he often joined the "under five years ordained" group. It is said that he much preferred suppers to meetings, but that he never stood on ceremony and, after a meal for example, would always be involved with the tidying and washing-up.

His vision for the Church was very much a product of the Council, but he had a vision ahead of his time, and he wanted collaboration between clergy and laity to be at the heart of church life. He urged his parishioners to be more friendly and non-judgemental towards outsiders. He believed firmly in the work of pastoral councils, and he reorganized the Diocesan Pastoral Council and set up the Council of Laity. At diocesan functions, he tried to speak with as many people as possible, talking with them easily and often being the last to leave! In particular, he was notably at ease with young people, playfully encouraging those seeking suitable spouses to pray to the Archangel Raphael, the patron of "happy meetings".

Griffiths' predecessor as bishop had an auxiliary whom Griffiths inherited: Bishop Owen Swindlehurst, Titular Bishop of Cuncacestre, auxiliary of Hexham and Newcastle and known as the Bishop of Chester-le-Street. Swindlehurst died on 28 August 1995, just three years into Griffiths' twelve-year episcopacy. Griffiths celebrated his Requiem and Bishop Lindsay preached. Swindlehurst was buried in Washington, just outside Sunderland, but significantly he was not replaced, so Griffiths set about reorganizing the administration of his diocese, which was, and is, huge, stretching from the River Tees in the south to the Scottish border. He divided the diocese into regions and appointed a number of vicars general to work alongside him and deputize for him.

But, as we have noted, Griffiths was not just an administrator; he had a well-developed pastoral side too and was involved in a number of notable activities. Perhaps first and foremost was his public commitment to young people, no doubt stemming, in part, from his time at Ampleforth as a schoolmaster.

Formally he was the representative of the Catholic bishops for young people. In his own diocese, he established (in 1994) a Youth Ministry Team (YMT), which aims to help young people discover their unique value and reach their full potential. Griffiths was clearly inspired by the Second Vatican Council's decree on the Apostolate of the Laity, which declared: "The young should become the first apostles of the young in direct contact with them, exercising the apostolate by themselves, among themselves, taking account of their social environment."[11] School missions proclaiming the gospel message in a lively, modern and interesting way, residential retreats and local youth ministry were some of the activities of the YMT. A youth village was established near Consett, which was subsequently renamed the Emmaus Village and provides a residential centre for young people, staffed by "gap year" teams.

One story which illustrates Griffiths' commitment to the young is that "when Pope John Paul II convened the World Youth Day in Rome, Ambrose travelled to Rome on a coach with the young people from his diocese. Quite oblivious to the inevitable noise around him he would put his head down and sleep, waking refreshed and ready to engage with his travelling companions."[12] It is perhaps no surprise that Bishop Griffiths was dubbed "bishop for the young".

A second important strand of his work was an interest in, and a commitment to, charismatic renewal. Charisms are special gifts of the Holy Spirit, over and above those strictly necessary for salvation. They are given to individuals or groups for the benefit of the Church and the world. Charismatic renewal movements emphasize the recognition and use of these charisms, which include healing, prophecy and speaking in tongues, to mention just a few. Pentecostal Christians emphasize baptism in the Spirit above all else, but within the Catholic Church there has been talk of "renewal" since the 1960s, with the "Called and Gifted" scheme in the UK perhaps being the most well known.

Originally, Griffiths said he did not know much about charismatic renewal and that it was not really "his thing", but one evening at Ampleforth, when he was procurator, he was emotionally and spiritually very low. He had heard that there was a charismatic group staying at

Ampleforth for the weekend, and he crept into the back of their meeting and sat down. Fr Sean Conaty was speaking, and Griffiths reported that, as he listened and looked around at the attentiveness of the people, suddenly a deep peace came over him. He said it was as if a light had gone on deep within him, and from then on he was a different person from the one who had crept into that meeting.[13] When Bishop Langton Fox, the liaison bishop to CCR (Catholic Charismatic Renewal), died, Cardinal Hume appointed Griffiths to be the new liaison bishop. It is said that although he was very supportive of CCR he retained some scepticism, especially concerning speaking in tongues. He felt that the benefits of renewal should be for all and that "tongues" put some people off.

Thirdly, Bishop Griffiths should be noted for his pastoral approach and that, even as bishop, he continued to show compassion and understanding towards individuals. I think this was sometimes misunderstood by the press. It is surely the case that "controversial bishop" is a more headline-grabbing epithet than "bishop who tried to explore possibilities within the rules"! In 1991, Griffiths invited divorced Catholics to Newcastle Cathedral, and at a special service acknowledged that divorce was on the increase, that divorce amongst Catholics was on the increase too. He expressed regret and asked forgiveness that the Church had often failed divorcees when they most needed support.

The Northern Echo reported that "the Roman Catholic Church has always rejected divorce", believing that once a marriage has taken place it should be for life,[14] but this is not strictly correct. Rather, problems arise when divorced Catholics remarry and thereby exclude themselves from the sacraments. Griffiths has, as far as I know, never rejected the teaching of the Church, or advocated communion for the remarried, but he has publicly supported further study of the problem by the bishops. He said: "We bishops in this country haven't the power to make a decision, but there is no harm in further theological investigation."[15] A deeper understanding of the theology of marriage is required.

It may be said that Griffiths exercised a little foresight, since Pope Francis has, on more than one occasion, suggested that the Church's stance might soften and that "the help of the sacraments" might be given to those in "irregular family situations". The Pope and many of the bishops recognize the need to support and integrate divorced and remarried Catholics into the life of the Church.

Similarly, Griffiths was again (wrongly in my view) dubbed as controversial when he suggested that the days of priestly celibacy could be numbered, and priests could possibly be married men. The context of the remark, which was rather overlooked, was that married men might be ordained *if there were insufficient clergy to celebrate the Eucharist*. He actually said, "celibacy is an excellent principle but sharing the Eucharist is more important. Therefore if we have not got enough priests left then we will have to ordain married men." Again, at the Amazon Synod of Bishops in November 2019 it was emphasized that priestly celibacy was a matter of discipline or law rather than a matter of doctrine or faith, and Pope Francis appeared to suggest that there could be changes to this discipline, particularly where there was a shortage of priests. Having said that he (the Pope) also seemed to suggest that the time for such changes had not yet arrived and there were no explicit references to changing the laws on priestly celibacy in the post-synodal documents. As I suggested above, Griffiths' greatest gift was perhaps his orthodox stance, a holding fast to the faith whilst at the same time extending compassion and mercy to persons as individuals.

When he reached the age of seventy-five (in December 2003), Bishop Griffiths offered his resignation to the Pope as requested (but not legally required) by canon law,[16] and on 26 March 2004 he retired from the see and returned to St Mary's in Leyland, Lancashire. Despite being a former abbot and bishop, he took on the role of assistant priest, under the priest who had previously been his assistant. With humility, but not without humour, he said that the post of assistant priest was still one he had not yet held, and he was longing to try it! He preferred to be addressed as Father, rather than anything more elevated, and he involved himself in visiting, counselling and as a chaplain to the local primary school. The people of Leyland were delighted to have him back. Indeed his warmth and his humour were often noted, and it was said that he could always see the funny side of things. It is even suggested that, as a young monk, his hilarity sometimes caused a disturbance in the choir or the refectory and earned him the gentle censure of his superiors!

Following his retirement from Hexham and Newcastle, he was awarded the honorary degree of DCL (Doctor of Civil Law) by Northumbria University. The university's vice-chancellor, Professor Kel Fidler, said:

> Bishop Ambrose Griffiths is an excellent role model for our graduates. He is a brilliant scholar with an analytic mind but understands how true success can only be achieved by working with people. This is a fantastic message for our graduates as they embark on their careers.[17]

Teresa Smith, a friend of Bishop Ambrose, recalled: "He was so pleased and it was the only time that I ever saw him look like 'the cat that got the cream'. He laughed heartily when I told him this, but he did not deny it."[18]

In January 2011, Griffiths was diagnosed with acute myeloid leukaemia, which was terminal, although it is said that those who visited him during his final illness found him joyful, efficient, even optimistic, comforting those who had come to comfort him. He was admitted to hospital after Easter that year, where he remained for a month, but when it became evident that there was no more that the doctors could do, he returned home to Leyland to die. The weekend after his return he attended Sunday Mass in a wheelchair and was determined to thank individually all those who had sent him cards and good wishes. Towards the very end, his family prayed the Office for him, and the monks offered Mass in his room. Eventually he needed more care than could be provided at home, and he was transferred to a local hospice for the very last few days of his life. He died in Leyland on 14 June 2011, aged eighty-two.

His Requiem Mass and funeral took place in St Mary's Cathedral, Newcastle, on 1 July 2011. The principal celebrant, Bishop Séamus Cunningham, Griffiths' successor after Bishop Dunn, was joined by Archbishop Vincent Nichols, Archbishop of Westminster, His Excellency Antonio Mennini, the Apostolic Nuncio, nine bishops, two abbots and over 100 priests, not to mention civic dignitaries and lay people who filled the cathedral to capacity.

In his homily, Séamus Cunningham recalled:

> I visited him just a few weeks ago and he knew that he had only a short time left and was dying as he had lived—full of gratitude and hope.... His infectious enthusiasm meant that his ministry as bishop of our diocese was a time of great blessing for us.... He had a special gift of getting alongside young people and inspiring them to pass on their faith.... The memory of his humility remains with us as an example of how authority is best exercised and how leadership must always be shaped by kindness.

Archbishop Patrick Kelly said: "Bishop Ambrose blessed the diocese of Liverpool in the parish of St Mary's Leyland, and blessed us again by dying in serenity and peace in our midst."

Following the final commendation, Bishop Ambrose's body was taken back to Ampleforth for burial in the crypt below the abbey church.

Notes

1. "A Brother's Memories" on the Catholic Charismatic Renewal website, <http://www.ccr.org.uk/old/archive/gn1109/g01.htm>, accessed 2 November 2021.
2. *The Daily Telegraph*, 31 August 2011.
3. Michael J. Walsh, *The Westminster Cardinals* (London: Burns & Oates, 2008), p. 197.
4. *The Ampleforth Journal* 115 (2011).
5. Ibid.
6. *Rule of Saint Benedict*, Chapter II, "What Kind of Man the Abbot should be".
7. *The Daily Telegraph*, 31 August 2011.
8. *The Ampleforth Journal* II:44 and I:80 (Spring 1991).
9. *The Daily Telegraph*, 31 August 2011.
10. See ibid.
11. *Apostolicam Actuositatem*, 12, in Austin Flannery OP, *Vatican Council II: The Conciliar and Postconciliar Documents*, Vol. I (New York: Costello Publishing, 1975, 1996), p. 780.
12. *The Ampleforth Journal* 115 (2011).
13. See "Pat Kennedy remembers" on the Catholic Charismatic Renewal website, <http://www.ccr.org.uk/old/archive/gn1109/g01.htm>, accessed 2 November 2021.
14. *Northern Echo*, 26 March 2001.
15. *Catholic Herald*, 17 September 1999.
16. *Code of Canon Law* (CIC), §401.
17. *Northern Echo*, 9 December 2004.
18. "My Friend Bishop Ambrose" on the Catholic Charismatic Renewal website, <http://www.ccr.org.uk/old/archive/gn1109/g01.htm>, accessed 2 November 2021.

12

Kevin John Dunn (2004–8)

Kevin Dunn, affectionately dubbed "the smiling bishop", was born in Newcastle under Lyme in Staffordshire on 9 July 1950. His father was Stephen Thomas Dunn (d. 2000), who was a pottery designer who later worked for the Michelin tyre company. His mother was Catherine (née Brennan), known as Cath. He had five siblings: sisters Elizabeth, Mary and Julia and brothers Stephen and Peter. He remained very close to his mother and his family throughout his life and even as bishop was well known in Clayton, as he would regularly return to Newcastle under Lyme to visit his mother.

He went to a number of schools: firstly, to St Mary's Primary School and from there to St Patrick's Secondary School. He then studied for a time with the Salvatorian Fathers at Christleton Hall near Chester before finally going to Cotton College to study for his A levels.

After Cotton, and having been impressed by his parish priest, who drove an old Ford car, Dunn went to the Birmingham archdiocesan seminary at Oscott to study for the priesthood. The seminary at Oscott was established in 1794. At first, it was a school for clerical students and lay pupils, and as a matter of fact in the college's infancy there were more lay students than clerics. In 1805, Francis Martyn was ordained priest, the first person since the Reformation to receive all his clerical education in England. In 1808, the lay governors of the college handed it over to the Vicar Apostolic of the Midland District, the forerunner of Birmingham diocese (the archdiocese was not created until 1911).

Following the completion of the new buildings in 1838, the college moved to a new site, so-called "New Oscott" on the Chester Road in Sutton Coldfield. Lay students and clerical students continued to be educated side by side until 1893, when Oscott closed for a time before becoming a seminary in the strict sense in 1897. When Dunn arrived (it is recorded at the college that he arrived on 10 September 1969), the college was thriving, Fr (later Bishop) Francis Thomas was rector and the college had just recently undergone the upheaval of changing from a liturgy that was all in Latin to a post-Conciliar English liturgy.

Dunn was ordained priest on 17 January 1976, at Our Lady and St Werbergh's Church at Clayton, Newcastle under Lyme. His first appointment was as assistant priest at St Patrick's Church, Walsall, and he was chaplain to Stuart Bathurst High School. From there, he went on to the Sacred Heart in Aston, living next door to the Aston Villa football ground. A mission was established at Aston as early as 1897, but the church dates from 1923-34, designed by George Bernard Cox of Harrison Cox architects in Birmingham. The church was constructed from brindle brick, laid in Flemish bond, with stone dressings under a clay pantile roof. The interior is richly decorated with marbles, mosaics and coloured glass.

Dunn is also particularly remembered for his work as chaplain to the Anglo-Caribbean community in Birmingham between 1980 and 1987. Alongside the quiet, steady work that he did, getting to know people and building community, he is also remembered for his involvement in, or rather his work in the face of, the "Handsworth riots". There were riots in Handsworth in 1981, 1985, 1991, 2005 and 2011, so it can be readily seen that the racial tension there is an ever-present problem. The 1981 riots were characterized by the Scarman Report as copycat riots following other disturbances in Brixton (London), Toxteth (Liverpool), Moss Side (Manchester) and elsewhere, although the position is certainly more nuanced than this.

The 1985 riots which took place from 9-11 September were ostensibly sparked by the arrest of a man at the Acapulco Cafe and a police raid on the Villa Cross public house. The police were attacked, property was looted and even bombs were detonated. Two brothers were burnt to death in the post office that they ran and there was a significant number of injuries. The more serious cause of the violence was ongoing and underlying racial tension between the local ethnic minority communities and the police. Very high unemployment amongst the black and Asian population was significant too.

Although expressing his shock at the events, Dunn found himself in the centre of a political and media storm. His first task was to visit his flock, some of whom had passed through the area on their way back from evening Mass. Then he met with local clergy to find a common stance, build bridges and calm things down. He later said to the *Catholic Herald* that "An enormous amount of work has already been done to calm things down."[1] He would also later emphasize that the most "ordinary people" played no part in the riots and that they were caused by a subculture alienated from society and church. But he significantly taught that this was not somebody else's problem, or that it was a situation for "experts" to solve the problems, but rather the opposite:

> Until every Christian acknowledges a positive obligation in the realm of race relations as they exist here and now in Britain, there will unquestionably be more riots, more bitterness and more indifference on the part of those who "do not want to know".[2]

The situation must have been a frightening and challenging one, but Dunn was subsequently praised for his prominent part in the aftermath of the riots.

In 1986, Dunn moved to Our Lady of the Angels and St Peter in Chains, in Stafford, a church which once had Fr Christopher Tolkien, son of the famous Catholic author J. R. R. Tolkien, as parish priest. While in Stafford, Dunn also served as chaplain to Stoke Infirmary and Stafford University. In the end, he would only stay at Our Lady's for two years, as in 1988 he was sent to "the Angelicum" in Rome to pursue further studies.

The Pontifical University of Thomas Aquinas (PUST), known colloquially as the Angelicum, is the Dominican university in Rome, situated at Santa Sabina. It has its origins in the thirteenth century but was significantly reformed in 1577 and 1963. While in Rome, Dunn studied canon law and was awarded his Doctorate in Canon Law (JCD) in 1991.

On his return from Rome, Dunn became parish priest at St Austin's, Stafford. Stafford was a local Catholic stronghold in the penal years, being the place of the martyrdom of Blessed Robert Sutton on 27 July 1588. Sutton was an Oxford graduate and a former Anglican minister who converted to Catholicism and was trained at the English College in Douai. He was ordained priest on 22 February 1578 and returned to England. He laboured "strenuously and holily in the Lord's vineyard"[3] but was captured in the house of Erasmus Wolsey in Stafford and, after a time in jail in London, was returned to Stafford and executed. A Catholic chapel was built in Stafford as soon as it was legally permitted.

This original chapel soon proved too small and was extended and remodelled in the Gothic style in 1814. The congregation continued to grow, and in the end a new church, designed by E. W. Pugin, son of the more famous A. W. N. Pugin, was built in 1861–2 in the Gothic Revival style. By 1994, some renovations were required, and Fr Dunn inaugurated an extensive restoration programme. In a first phase (1995), the fabric of the building was put in good order, then in a second phase (1998) the interior was redecorated. The false ceiling installed in the nave in 1973 was removed to create a light and high vista. The altar canopy was removed and new lighting installed.

If this work was not enough, Dunn also began to teach canon law at the seminary at Oscott. Seminary teaching brings a priest into contact with a wide variety of clergy, from different dioceses, and with the Catholic hierarchy too. Many seminary rectors go on to be bishops, and although Dunn was not the rector, it is certainly not unreasonable to suppose that this spell at Oscott contributed in a significant way to his future preferment. In 1993, Dunn was appointed episcopal vicar for religious in the archdiocese of Birmingham, and eight years later, in 2001, he was appointed as full-time episcopal vicar for the areas of Wolverhampton, Walsall, the Black Country and Worcestershire. In 2002, he was appointed a canon of St Chad's Cathedral, a member of the Metropolitan Chapter of St Chad, and joined the bishop's council.

On 20 March 2004, fittingly the feast of St Cuthbert, Dunn was appointed as the twelfth Bishop of Hexham and Newcastle by Pope John Paul II. He was ordained bishop in the cathedral on the feast of St Bede, 25 May 2004, by his predecessor, Bishop Ambrose Griffiths, assisted by Bishops Patrick Kelly (Archbishop of Liverpool) and Vincent Nichols (at the time Archbishop of Birmingham). It was reported that he nearly missed his own ordination and enthronement because, when he arrived at the cathedral without a ticket, the security staff, not knowing who he was, initially refused to let him in![4]

Despite his short tenure, he achieved much as a bishop and quickly became involved in a number of areas. In 2005, he reorganized the diocesan administration, introducing five pastoral vicariates, each with an episcopal vicar whose role was to advise and assist him in the diocese. He appointed a new personal assistant and a diocesan chancellor. He was also responsible for changing the whole form of parish visitations within the diocese and, together with his council, he encouraged parishes throughout the diocese to use the episcopal visitation as an opportunity to see how well the parish community worked together, and what could be done to improve those areas that needed development.

On a hands-on or more down-to-earth level, like his predecessor, he was particularly involved with young people; indeed on the day of his ordination as bishop he was presented with a book of welcome, to which every school in the diocese had contributed. It was always on display in Bishop's House. He attended the World Youth Day held in Cologne. He regularly went on the diocesan pilgrimage to Lourdes, encouraging young people to develop their faith. He gave his full support to the Church's work with young people, and he supported the diocese's Catholic schools and the development of the "Youth Village" in the diocese. On one occasion he surprised teachers by presenting a huge bag of conkers for the children, which he had collected from his garden.

At an administrative level too, his work with the Catholic Bishops' Conference of England and Wales reflected his concerns for schools and young people. He was formally a member of the Catholic Education and Formation Committee; he was chair of the Board of Religious Studies of the Catholic Education Service. He sat on the committee for the Catholic Office for the Protection of Children and Vulnerable Adults (COPCA)[5] and, for the record, he chaired the canon law working party.

Dunn worked hard to encourage Catholics in the North-East, particularly by emphasizing the Catholic history and heritage of that area and promoting the history of, and the devotion to, the local saints. It is said he was always talking of Cuthbert, Aidan and Bede. He promoted the work of refurbishment of St Aidan's church on Holy Island (Lindisfarne), mounting the campaign to have that little church restored and enlarged. In 2006, Dunn led a pilgrimage "in the footsteps of St Cuthbert" to the Farne Islands and, in 2007, he welcomed both the Titular Bishop of Lindisfarne and the Papal Nuncio to the island. Cuthbert, having spent twelve years on Lindisfarne in obedience to Abbot Eata, living the community life with his brothers, felt he must yield to the call of the desert and take up the solitary life. He went first, in 676, to Cuthbert's Isle (Hobthrush Isle), connected to Lindisfarne by a causeway at low tide but an island at high tide. Thereafter he went to the more remote Isle of Farne, several miles off the coast of Northumberland, where he remained for nine years. He built a round house, digging deep into the rock so that its floor was below ground level. He also built a small cabin near the landing place, on the seaward side of the island, where visiting monks might stay. In 684, when Eata became Bishop of Hexham, Cuthbert became Bishop of Lindisfarne, but he eventually returned to the Farne Islands, where he died in 687.

Dunn's love of the local saints also had liturgical consequences and he promulgated a new diocesan lectionary and supplement to the Roman missal "*Ad Experimentum*" with appropriate texts for the lives of the saints of the North-East of England. He was also involved in a collaborative project and instrumental in raising money (over £2 million) for the establishment of the Bede Chair of Catholic Theology, the first such chair since the Reformation, at (what was to become) the Centre for Catholic Studies at the University of Durham. The Vatican Congregation for Catholic Education commended the efforts and the care that had been shown in this project. Since Dunn's death, an annual lecture in his memory—The Bishop Dunn Memorial Lecture—is held each year. In the *Catholic Herald*, Archbishop Vincent Nichols described this as a "lasting tribute to Kevin".

Turning to vocations, Dunn was very active in promoting vocations to the priesthood. He appointed a diocesan promoter of vocations to work alongside the vocations director and opened a new "House of Hospitality" in Penshaw, as a place where enquirers could live for a period of time. There was just one permanent deacon in the diocese when Dunn arrived, and he encouraged this vocation too, ordaining the first "group" of deacons for the diocese in 2005, with more in 2006 and 2007.

As well as overtly Catholic witness, Dunn was actively involved in ecumenical endeavours. He regularly met with the North-East Churches Together group, of which he was, for a time, deputy moderator. He is particularly remembered for organizing a trip to Rome for local church leaders, the highlight of which was an audience with Pope Benedict XVI, who greeted them personally. The group also met Cardinal Kasper, head of the Pontifical Council for the Promotion of Christian Unity. On a less exalted note, Bishop Dunn was a keen golfer, and he organized an annual golf tournament with the Anglican clergy and their bishop, (biblical scholar) Tom Wright from the diocese of Durham.

Towards the end of 2007, Dunn's health began to deteriorate and his last official engagement, on 30 November, was when he visited the SVP's Ozanam House in Newcastle. He was admitted to hospital for almost a month. On 5 February 2008, he was re-admitted to the Freeman Hospital in Newcastle and diagnosed with pneumonia. On 8 February, he was moved to the intensive care unit, and although the stability of his condition was maintained in the main, his overall condition steadily deteriorated. Nevertheless, the hospital staff did an excellent job keeping him comfortable and at the last his family, the Vicar General Canon Séamus Cunningham and clergy from the bishop's council gathered to pray the prayers for the dying.

Dunn died peacefully, in his sleep, at around 9.30 p.m. on Saturday 1 March 2008, aged fifty-seven years.

His body was brought into Newcastle Cathedral on 10 March at 7 p.m., so that parishioners and clergy could pay their last respects. A Mass was celebrated, followed by a prayer vigil which ended with night prayer, or Compline, at 10 p.m. His funeral and Requiem Mass took place the following day at noon. The chief celebrant was Patrick Kelly, Archbishop of Liverpool, who was joined by thirty-two bishops, archbishops and the Apostolic Nuncio. Additionally, there were some 245 priests and deacons from Hexham and Newcastle and other dioceses. There was a large ecumenical presence too, including the Anglican Bishops of Durham and of Newcastle and representatives from other faith groups. Finally, there was a number of civic dignitaries, including MPs, and, of course, many of Dunn's family and friends, including his mother, Cath, then aged eighty-eight.

In his homily, Vincent Nichols, then Archbishop of Birmingham, praised Bishop Dunn's interest in, and devotion to, the Catholic heritage of the North-East and the local saints. He said Dunn "was in the very best sense, father to the diocese, although his time here has been short. A canon lawyer by training, yet he had such a big pastoral heart."[6] After the Requiem Mass, Dunn's body was interred in the crypt of the cathedral.

Bishop Dunn was perhaps the first Catholic bishop in England to have his death marked by a podcast, posted on the diocesan website, with the choir of St Mary's Cathedral singing the hauntingly beautiful *"Libera me"* from Gabriel Fauré's setting of the Requiem Mass.

All the many tributes paid to Bishop Dunn at his death attest to his warmth and humanity. He had "a marvellous ability to put people at their ease, to create around him a sense of belonging, a family sense which was so precious".[7] The Newcastle Central MP at the time, Jim Cousins, who was a close friend of the bishop, said that he would be sorely missed. "He was an important leader and not just of the Catholic faith but for the broader faith community on Tyneside. I had a huge respect for the humanity of his views and sensitive way that they were always expressed."[8] Rabbi Dovid Lewis of Newcastle upon Tyne said: "The wider world of Christendom and all religions have lost a faithful shepherd and leader. He was a man who was able to transcend religious boundaries and see the human being behind the mask. As a religious man I appreciated his thoughtfulness, but as a fellow citizen of this world I enjoyed his humour and his smile." Tajik Malik, president of the Newcastle Mosque and Islamic Centre in Malvern Street, said: "He was an extremely nice person, he always tried to bring people together and to bring peace. We worked together and I always found he was extremely nice to work with and easy to talk to. He will be missed."[9]

Notes

[1] *Catholic Herald*, 20 September 1985.
[2] Ibid..
[3] John Hungerford Pollen, *Acts of the English Martyrs Hitherto Unpublished* (London: Burns & Oates, 1891), p. 324.
[4] See *The Times*, 11 March 2008.
[5] See *The Independent*, 25 March 2008.
[6] *Catholic Herald*, 14 March 2008.
[7] Ibid..
[8] Quoted in the *Catholic Herald*, 7 March 2008.
[9] *Evening Chronicle*, 3 March 2008.

1 3
Séamus Cunningham (2009–19)

Bishop Dunn was succeeded by Séamus Cunningham, who became the thirteenth Bishop of Hexham and Newcastle. He was born on 7 July 1942 at Castlebar in Co. Mayo, Ireland, into a devout and close-knit family. He was one of ten children (two of his sisters became nuns) and his father was a farmer. He recalls that, when he was out in the fields, on hearing the Angelus bell, his father would take off his hat and pray. "For us, God wasn't somewhere up in the clouds, he was very real and very close."

He was educated at local Irish schools including St Nathy's College, Ballaghaderreen, where his episcopal predecessor and great uncle, Bishop James Cunningham (ninth of Hexham and Newcastle) had also briefly studied. The school moved to Ballaghaderreen in 1893 and took over a military barracks purchased by the diocese from the War Office. Under the leadership of the local bishop, the school flourished in the early part of the twentieth century and is now (following various amalgamations) one of the largest schools in the West of Ireland. It was during his time at school that young Séamus discerned a vocation to the priesthood, a niggling away down the years. He recalls that, although his mother warned him of the realities of clerical loneliness and the challenge of celibacy, his parents supported him completely.

And so, after his schooling, Cunningham went to study for the priesthood in the far South-East of Ireland at St John's College, Waterford. Founded in 1807 by Bishop John Power, the new college was formed by merging two older establishments and was originally located at Manor Hill, Waterford, housed in a mansion formerly belonging to the Wyse family. Later, a new building was constructed at John's Hill. Cunningham studied diploma courses in philosophy and theology and would also have enjoyed academic links with the pontifical faculty at Maynooth. Cunningham recalls:

> I was lucky. The moment I walked through the seminary gates I knew it was for me. There was a terrific sense of community among the students. The discipline was very strict. The staff could be quite distant but they were men of prayer. It laid a rock foundation just as my mother and father had laid a rock foundation.[1]

The seminary closed in 1999. Cunningham was ordained priest, for the diocese of Hexham and Newcastle, on 12 June 1966 by Bishop Michael Russell, Bishop of Waterford and Lismore.

Very shortly afterwards, he travelled from Waterford to the parish of Our Lady and St Joseph, called Brooms, at Leadgate, near Consett in north-west Durham, to be the new curate. It was the first time Cunningham had left Ireland and the first time he had travelled by aeroplane! The first Saturday afternoon that he was there he planned to do some pastoral visiting, but it was gently suggested (by Fr Joe Park, his new parish priest) that he might not be welcome. Despite all the flags and bunting Cunningham had not realized it was the day of the memorable football World Cup final between England and West Germany!

The church of our Blessed Lady and St Joseph is a large Victorian church, designed by E. W. Pugin and built between 1866 and 1869, which replaced a smaller chapel there. The church served a large immigrant Catholic community brought to the area by the ironworks and other industry at Consett. Cunningham would have learnt his trade there, celebrating the sacraments and becoming involved in the life of the community. In 1971, he was sent to English Martyrs in Newcastle, a tall, brick-clad church built in 1963. It is surely a matter of taste, but some have observed that the striking interior displays a creative use of concrete.

The following year Cunningham travelled south to Bayswater, west London, to study religious education and catechetics at the then new, but now closed, Corpus Christi College. This college was established in 1965 with the support of Cardinal Heenan and with Hubert Richards as principal. Within a year, there were complaints that the teaching at the college was far too theologically radical, and indeed the evening lectures started to attract huge crowds. The vice-principal resigned in 1971 and the rest of the staff later the same year after Heenan had refused to approve the list of visiting speakers.[2] A new principal was appointed, but the college closed in 1975.

Nevertheless, and despite what must have been a turbulent year "down south", Cunningham completed his studies and returned to Newcastle Cathedral, where he was based, but travelled throughout the diocese visiting schools and colleges. In 1976, he succeeded Fr Leo Pyle as director of religious education in the diocese, and he also became chaplain to St Mary's Teacher Training College in Fenham.

In 1984, he went to the diocesan seminary at Ushaw to act as spiritual director for the students there. This is a key role in a seminary, since it is laid down in canon law that every seminary is to have a rector, a vice-rector if circumstances warrant it, a financial administrator and at least one spiritual director (although students are also free to approach other priests).[3] Of course there are to be professors and lecturers, but these are not legally stipulated in the way that the spiritual director is. Furthermore, following the publication of *Pastores Dabo Vobis* by Pope John Paul II (March 1992), new norms for the training of priests were laid down and formation was to be understood as resting upon four fundamentals: human, intellectual, pastoral and spiritual. Hence the role of the spiritual director is a significant one, for he has the responsibility of shaping and forming his students.

In 1987, Cunningham returned to Newcastle Cathedral as administrator and parish priest, a role he would fulfil for the next decade. Shortly after his arrival, he was appointed a canon and joined the cathedral chapter.

In 1998, he took a short sabbatical in the United States before returning to care for St Oswin's in Tynemouth and St Mary's Cullercoats.

In 2001, Bishop Griffiths appointed him one of the four new vicars general.

In 2004, Bishop Dunn promoted Canon Cunningham to be his sole vicar general, and effectively his deputy. He worked closely with Bishop Dunn throughout his short time as bishop and was present with him, and his family, throughout Dunn's illness, until his death on 1 March 2008.

Cunningham was appointed diocesan administrator the following day. On 21 December, "just after lunch", Cunningham received a telephone call asking him to visit the Papal Nuncio in London to discuss confidential matters. Cunningham was expecting to discuss, or to be told, who the next bishop would be. His own elevation had never crossed his mind, as he considered himself to be neither an academic nor a "high-flyer", and he recalls being in a state of shock.

On 9 January 2009, Pope Benedict made the public announcement that Cunningham would be the next Bishop of Hexham and Newcastle. Cunningham observed:

> Although I was surprised to be asked to undertake this task, I am glad that the diocese will not have to face another change of style within very few years. I hope to start by continuing Bishop Kevin's initiatives before seeking anew what will be best at this time to meet the many challenges in spreading the Gospel today and working with the other church bodies and civil authorities.

On 20 March 2009, the feast of St Cuthbert, he was ordained bishop and installed in the cathedral at the hands of Archbishop Patrick Kelly, Archbishop of Liverpool, who enjoined the new bishop to "be joyful". Kelly was assisted by Bishop Ambrose Griffiths OSB, Bishop Emeritus of Hexham and Newcastle, and Bishop Michael Campbell, coadjutor Bishop of Lancaster. Apart from one who had died, all of Bishop Cunningham's siblings attended his episcopal ordination along with most of his twenty-nine nephews and nieces and a crowd of other relatives from Ireland: over 100 in number.

Bishop Cunningham had moved from the presbytery in Tynemouth to the manorial bishop's residence on the western outskirts of Newcastle and Cunningham recalls many of them watching the rugby—the Grand Slam. "It was terrific, so much joy and excitement."

Having served in the diocese for so long, the new Bishop Cunningham was under no illusion about the demands of the job. He was well aware of the social, spiritual and material deprivation in the area, and the declining church attendance and vocations to the priesthood. He recognized that the challenges were huge. He was equally clear about his own role and the role of his clergy. "Let's face it, there are many things which lay people do much better than priests and that sets me and other priests free to do what our ordination called us to do—to preach the word of God, to celebrate the sacraments and to care for people."

In January 2010, the year after his episcopal ordination, Bishop Cunningham made his first *ad limina* visit to Rome, along with Archbishop Vincent Nichols and six other bishops. This was the first visit by English and Welsh bishops since the election of Pope Benedict XVI. These visits are usually every five years (quinquennial), and the bishops travel *ad limina apostolorum*, "to the threshold of the apostles", to venerate the tombs of St Peter and St Paul, thereby implicitly accepting the Pope as St Peter's successor, the universal pastor of the Church. The bishops traditionally meet the Pope collectively and individually, to give an account of their dioceses.

Much of the discussion at that visit was about the shortage of priestly vocations. Bishop Kieran Conry, then Bishop of Arundel and Brighton, revealed that the English and Welsh bishops' report had "made clear that we are facing challenges that the Church in the west is generally facing. These include a more strident secularism and atheism alongside a declining number of priests which is having an effect on parish life." John Rawsthorne, then Bishop of Hallam, also emphasized during the visit that a shortage of priests would be a key issue, and he reported the bishops' wish to consult with the Pope on the matter.

Also during the 2010 *ad limina* visit and in the light at that time of the imminent beatification of (now St) John Henry Newman, the English and Welsh bishops asked to visit the places especially connected with the life of the cardinal. They visited the Chapel of the Three Kings, now inside the Missio headquarters but at the time the chapel of the Collegio di Propaganda Fide, where Newman was ordained priest by Cardinal Giacomo Filippo Fransoni on 30 May 1847. They also visited the Newman Chapel in the same building where Newman first celebrated Mass, on the following Thursday, the feast of Corpus Christi. In Newman's time, this was the Jesuits' chapel, and Newman offered the Mass on an altar above the shrine of St Hyacinth, not far from his room. This altar, which had been moved to the new Collegio Urbano on the Gianicolo, was recently returned to Propaganda Fide and placed in a chapel now dedicated to Newman.⁴

Of course, it was later that same year that Pope Benedict XVI made a state visit to the United Kingdom. The principal event was the beatification of Cardinal John Henry Newman in Cofton Park, Birmingham, on Sunday 19 September 2010. The Pope could have delegated this task to somebody else, but on account of his great admiration, and indeed affection, for the work of Newman, Pope Benedict undertook the task himself. The official announcement of the state visit recorded:

> Since the election of Pope Benedict XVI, in April 2005, all Beatification ceremonies, with a few exceptions in Rome, had been held in the diocese where the servant of God was either born, lived or died. It was the personal wish of Pope Benedict XVI to come to England to beatify Cardinal Newman in the Archdiocese of Birmingham.⁵

In his homily, Pope Benedict likened Newman to the saint-scholars of the North-East:

> Cardinal Newman is worthy to take his place in a long line of saints and scholars from these islands, St Bede, St Hilda, St Aelred, Blessed Duns Scotus, to name but a few. In Blessed John Henry, that tradition of gentle scholarship, deep human wisdom and profound love for the Lord has borne rich fruit, as a sign of the abiding presence of the Holy Spirit, deep within the heart of God's people, bringing forth abundant gifts of holiness.⁶

Pope Benedict did not visit the diocese of Hexham and Newcastle, but Bishop Cunningham attended the beatification Mass and the meeting of the Pope with the bishops of England, Scotland and Wales held at St Mary's College, Oscott (the seminary in Birmingham) later the same day. In his address, the Pope encouraged the bishops concerning two specific matters. First, that they should embrace the new (English) translation of the Roman Missal. The Pope encouraged the bishops to seize the opportunity that the new translation offered for in-depth catechesis on the Eucharist and renewed devotion in the manner of its celebration. Second, the Pontiff asked the bishops to be generous in the implementation of the Apostolic Constitution *Anglicanorum Coetibus*, which paved the way for the establishment of the Ordinariate of Our Lady of Walsingham in the UK. The Pope reminded the bishops that full ecclesial communion was the ultimate goal of all ecumenical activity: a goal for which all should pray and work.

Shortly before his retirement, Bishop Cunningham made a second *ad limina* visit to Rome in 2018 as part of a much larger group and was received along with the other bishops by Pope Francis, who does not (normally) receive bishops individually but meets them as a group. He exchanged views with them freely and encouraged and affirmed their ministries. It is perhaps interesting that the topic of priestly vocations was discussed again. *The Tablet* reported that Pope Francis "spoke of the encouragement he wishes to give priests today, who can sometimes feel vulnerable in the face of difficult circumstances, in a critical environment. The Pope added we are to live the gift of our faith with joy. Joy was his great emphasis. He explained that this joy is firmly rooted in our relationship with Jesus."[7]

As befitted his past experience, within the Catholic Bishops' Conference Cunningham had a particular involvement in the Department for Evangelisation and Catechesis (now renamed Evangelisation and Discipleship).

In June 2016, Cunningham celebrated the golden jubilee of his priestly ordination, and a special Mass was celebrated in Newcastle Cathedral with family and friends, clergy and laity from across the diocese. Fr Adrian Dixon preached the homily and reflected on the service offered by Bishop Séamus in his priestly ministry along with all the priests of the diocese. Fr Dixon also described Bishop Séamus as an accomplished mimic and underlined how the priest and the bishop imitate Christ, not just copying, but acting as a real *alter Christus*. In Bishop Séamus' ministry it has been, and is, Christ himself who acts. Bishop Séamus was also presented with a letter from Pope Francis, who wrote: "From the bottom of our hearts we want to sing the praises of God with you for the outstanding gift of his goodness."

In March 2017, the diocese of Hexham and Newcastle held its first Pope John Paul II Award ceremony in the Tyne Theatre and Opera House. Bishop Cunningham presented papal gold, silver and bronze awards to 120 young people, assisted by Fr Paul Farren, the founder of the award from Derry in Ireland, who presented accompanying certificates. The awards were presented for active engagement in the life of the community and society: putting faith into action. The challenge is to "go beyond your comfort zone on a journey of self-discovery". The administration of the awards also strengthened the link between churches and local secondary schools. Bishop Séamus himself wrote:

> I wholeheartedly welcome the introduction of the Pope John Paul II awards in our diocese. This award calls our young people to deepen their relationship with Christ and to live out their faith in generous service of others. The young people of our diocese are a great blessing and we need their unique gifts in our communities.

In June 2017, Bishop Cunningham visited Rome to ordain deacons at the Beda College. His homily to the about-to-be-ordained men and their supporters revealed something of his own spirituality. He told the men that, as deacons, they were to be evangelizers, heralds of the good news on the margins between the Church and the world, proclaiming the gospel message in the church and in the world. But, he went on to say, in order to evangelize the deacon must first be evangelized. He must hear the message himself. And this hearing is not just about the ears and the brain, as the message must penetrate the heart so that it can be announced joyfully to a waiting world. The message is spoken with conviction to those who wonder, spoken gently to the grieving and the sorrowful, and whispered into the ears of the sick and the dying. He went on to say that the charism of self-giving and eager availability lies at the heart of the spirituality of deacons, but I think we can see that this is no mere theological platitude, rather a lesson learnt first-hand, over many years as priest and bishop, by Cunningham himself. It clearly shows his own understanding of ministry and service.[8]

As is customary, Bishop Cunningham offered his resignation to Pope Francis on reaching his seventy-fifth birthday in July 2017. The Pope asked him to remain in office for a while, and it was not until February 2019 that his successor was announced. Hence Cunningham did not formally retire until 4 February 2019. In retirement Bishop Cunningham moved from Newcastle to Seaburn.

Later in the same month (22 February), a Mass of thanksgiving was celebrated in his honour in the cathedral. In the homily, Fr Peter Leighton described Cunningham, first and foremost, as a man of prayer, rooted and grounded in God's love: moreover, built on that solid foundation "love turn[s] into a well-directed and effective energy". Bishop Cunningham was described as a man who knew that for his actions to be effective, they must emerge from prayer, and he was also always encouraging his priests and people to a committed prayer life.

The preacher quoted St Peter's advice that shepherds should look after their flocks not just as a duty but because God wants it,[9] and suggested that Cunningham knew this and took it to heart. Cunningham responded with generous faithfulness to his appointment as bishop, not ruling and officiating simply as a duty. Retirement gifts were given to the bishop and in a vote of thanks he expressed his gratitude, humbled by the people's generosity, and he assured them, and the whole diocese, of his continued prayers.

Notes

1. *Northern Echo*, 2 April 2009.
2. See Michael J. Walsh, *The Westminster Cardinals* (London: Burns & Oates, 2008), p. 185.
3. See *Code of Canon Law* (CIC), §239.
4. See Brigitte Hoegemann, "Newman and Rome", in *John Henry Newman in His Time*, ed. Philippe Lefebvre and Colin Mason (Oxford: Family Publications, 2007), pp. 61–81, here at pp. 77–8.
5. Peter Jennings (ed.), *Benedict XVI and Blessed John Henry Newman: The State Visit 2010, the Official Record* (London: CTS, 2010), p. 39.
6. Pope Benedict, Cofton Park, 19 September 2010.
7. *The Tablet*, 1 October 2018.
8. See Séamus Cunningham, "Diaconate Ordinations Homily, 14 June 2017", *The Beda Review* (2016–17), pp. 22–5.
9. See 1 Peter 5:2.

1 4

Robert John Byrne (2019–)

Bishop Cunningham was succeeded by Bishop Robert Byrne CO of the Congregation of the Oratory. He was born on 22 September 1956 at Urmston. His father was Sydney Byrne, and his mother was Monica née Rigby. His uncle, Fr John Rigby, a priest in the Salford diocese, recalls that, influenced by him, he always wanted to be a priest. Byrne was educated at St Bede's College in Manchester, an independent Catholic school founded in 1876 by Herbert Vaughan (then Bishop of Salford). The school has a number of notable alumni, including over half a dozen bishops.

After St Bede's, Byrne went to King's College in London, where he read theology and gained a BD degree and the AKC (Associate of King's College) qualification.

As well as wanting to be a priest, Byrne sought a community life and thought, for a time, of being a Benedictine monk. However, on a visit to the Birmingham Oratory he was "captivated" by the Birmingham Oratorians, and he entered the Oratory in 1980 to begin his formation. He was professed on 30 September 1982. The constitution of the Oratory is a little unusual. It was originally established in Rome by St Philip Neri, who did not want to join, or even less to found, a religious order. Rather, he sought to rediscover the fervour of the early days of the Church, and he conceived of a group of secular priests living and working together, renewing the Church and serving the people: encouraging them to become saints in their own homes. From as early as 1552, Philip gathered a group of men around him, but a stable communal life did not begin until around 1564. In 1575, the community moved to the Chiesa Nuova and the Oratorians were approved by Pope Gregory XIII, who knew St Philip personally.

Significantly, Newman, following his conversion to Roman Catholicism (1845) and ordination to the priesthood (1847), sought some kind of religious identity. The Jesuits and the Dominicans were considered, but Cardinal Wiseman suggested the Congregation of the Oratory to Newman, who recognized the perfect compromise, if we may call it that, of secular priests living together in community. Newman also recognized that the Oratorian rule was rather more custom than strict injunction, which allowed him (with permission) to readily revise the rule for England. "He saw great possibilities in this free form of association, especially suitable for modern cities and for men of different capabilities."[1]

After a very brief novitiate and instruction from Fr Rossi of the Roman Oratory, Newman and his five companions, Frs St John, Dalgairns, Penny, Coffin and Stanton, were received into the Oratory and returned to England, establishing the first English Oratory at Maryvale in Birmingham. They arrived on 1 January 1848, and the chapel was formally opened on 2 February, the official founding date. The early history is well known and here is not the place to retell it, save to say that a second Oratory was established in London (the Brompton Oratory) the following year; but, despite Newman's wishes and intentions, an Oratory in Oxford was not established in his day.

As part of his formation, Byrne was sent to the Pontifical University of St Thomas (the *Angelicum*) in Rome, where he engaged in non-degree studies in the Faculty of Philosophy from 1981–2 and in the Faculty of Theology from 1982–4. He returned to Birmingham and was ordained as an Oratorian priest on 5 January 1985 in Edgbaston at the hands of Archbishop Maurice Couve de Murville. His first job, beyond his duties at the Oratory, was to act as chaplain to St Philip's College in Edgbaston.

St Aloysius' Church in Oxford is the principal Catholic church in central Oxford, designed by J. Hansom and built in 1875. It was, for the first hundred years or so of its existence, served by the Society of Jesus (or Jesuits) which established it. The Jesuits withdrew from the church in 1981, and priests of the archdiocese of Birmingham cared for the church and the parish until 1990, when Archbishop Couve de Murville asked the Birmingham Oratory if it could provide priests to run the Oxford parish.

In September 1990, Byrne moved from Birmingham with Fr Dominic Jacob CO to run the parish and establish a new Oratory in Oxford. Byrne was appointed parish priest. Shortly afterwards they were joined by a third Oratorian who was at that time a student priest: Richard Duffield CO. The work flourished and numbers increased until 1993, when the Oxford Oratory was established as an independent Oratorian Congregation with Byrne as the first provost, as Oratorians call their superior. It is worth noting that there is no central Oratorian authority as such: each congregation is a foundation by "pontifical right", although there is a Federation of the Oratory of St Philip which was established in 1942. In 2000, Byrne became secretary to the Permanent Deputation of the International Oratorian Federation, a post he held for eleven years.

Under Byrne, the Oxford Oratory flourished and grew. A rich liturgical tradition was established with a full complement of Catholic devotions and observances. Fine music and a very competent choir, which is very much part of the Oratorian tradition, was, and is, a noticeable feature of the Oxford Oratory. The liturgy centres on Solemn High Mass on a Sunday morning at 11 a.m. The liturgy is *novus ordo* Latin, with the choir singing a setting of the Kyrie, Sanctus and Agnus Dei and the congregation singing a plainsong Gloria (usually *de Angelis*), Credo and a hymn. Except in the case of solemnities and feasts, most of the other Masses in the week are *novus ordo* in English, but there are regular weekly Masses in Latin, both in the n*ovus ordo* and the extraordinary form. Indeed, Byrne has been noted as "a friend of the extraordinary form" and has presided at Solemn Masses in that form of the rite.

Byrne has been particularly noted for his prison ministry over thirty-five years or more. It started, he says, rather by accident, when the bishop rang the Birmingham Oratory (in 1987) and asked if it could provide a prison chaplain. He started at HMP Winson Green, a category B men's prison in Birmingham. He continued this work when he moved south, at Oxford prison until it closed in 1996, and then at HMP Bullingdon, a young offenders' institute near Bicester, which accommodates some 1,100 men. Byrne has said that prison ministry is very "raw". There are few niceties in prison, and much of the self-respect and pride of the prisoners has gone. Byrne particularly tries to take the light of Christ into the prison, conscious that he is an *alter Christus*, another Christ, bringing God's grace to those in need. On his translation to Hexham and Newcastle, Byrne has stated he would visit the prisons in the North-East: "I will be making it central to my work. I've already spoken to Bishop Séamus about it. It's something I'm concerned about," he said.

In January 2010, Byrne celebrated the silver jubilee of his ordination to the priesthood. A Solemn Mass was offered at Oxford Oratory. The setting was Haydn's *Mariazeller Messe* accompanied by strings and timpani! The then Provost of the London Oratory (Fr Ignatius Harrison) visited and preached and the Procurator General of the Confederation of the Oratory, Fr Eduardo Cerrato, sent special greetings, congratulating Fr Robert and thanking him for all his work.

Byrne served as provost in Oxford for some twenty years until 2011, when the Fathers of the Oratory elected Fr Daniel Seward CO to replace him. In 2012, Byrne was appointed national ecumenical officer and secretary to the Bishops' Conference Department of Dialogue and Unity. Two years earlier this department published "Meeting God in Friend and Stranger", which reminded Christians that they are called by their common baptism to foster understanding and mutual respect amongst themselves and with people of other religions. Some years later, in a "Vimeo video", Byrne outlined his hope for full and visible unity amongst all Christians, but recognizing that this was something of an (eschatological) ideal he emphasized that all Christians should talk to each other and that each can learn from the other. Each community, through its love of scripture and its tradition, can teach other communities, allowing us to reach out and spread the Christian message, he said.

On 15 March 2014, Byrne was appointed as Titular Bishop of Cuncacestre and Auxiliary Bishop of Birmingham, news which was communicated to him via the Papal Nuncio. He was ordained bishop at 11 a.m. on 13 May in St Chad's Cathedral, Birmingham, by Archbishop Bernard Longley (Birmingham) assisted by Bishop Michael Barber SJ (Bishop of Oakland, California) and Bishop Philip Pargeter (the Titular Bishop of Valentiniana, and former auxiliary bishop in Birmingham— Byrne's predecessor). Byrne is particularly noted for being the first Oratorian to be appointed bishop in England since 1874, when Fr Edward Bagshawe, of the London Oratory, was appointed the third Bishop of Nottingham. Bishop Robert remarked, "In the spirit of St

Philip Neri—the founder of the Oratory and a saint with a great sense of humour—I am committed to helping share the joy of the gospel message with others."

Archbishop Bernard Longley said:

> I am immensely grateful to Pope Francis for appointing Fr Robert Byrne Auxiliary Bishop of Birmingham. From his time at the Birmingham Oratory and as Provost of the Oxford Oratory, Fr Robert has come to know our archdiocese well. Having worked alongside him in recent years as the Bishops' Conference's ecumenical officer I know that he will bring considerable pastoral, theological and administrative skills to his new responsibilities as bishop. Above all I am grateful that he brings the spirituality of St Philip Neri, the founder of the Oratory, to enrich his ministry among us.

In his homily at the ordination, Cardinal Vincent Nichols especially asked for the blessings of St Philip Neri and (then) Blessed John Henry Newman, "of whom Father Robert is a true son".

Bishop Byrne was given special responsibility for the geographical areas of Birmingham and Worcester and took up residence at St Mary's College in Oscott. As a member of the Catholic Bishops' Conference of England and Wales, Bishop Byrne is a member of both the Department of Dialogue and Unity, where he served as secretary, and the Department of Life and Worship.

In 2016, Byrne attended the International Eucharistic Congress in Cebu City in the Philippines, and this inspired him to propose and organize a National Eucharistic Congress in Liverpool, called Adoremus. "I saw it could be an opportunity to renew our faith and our commitment in this country to the Eucharist," he said. The congress lasted for three days, and it is estimated that some 30,000 people were involved. In addition to the liturgies, there were speakers, symposia and an enormous procession of the Blessed Sacrament through the streets of Liverpool, stretching for some two kilometres. It was said to be the first such procession since 1908. On the main day 7,000 people, including almost 500 from the Birmingham archdiocese, packed into the ACC Liverpool Arena to hear the renowned speaker Bishop Barron from the US. Afterwards, Byrne said, "People went away from Adoremus in Liverpool deeply moved and wanting to spread the idea of Adoration, which brings us back to Christ and the mystery of the Mass."[2]

In 2018, Byrne joined a fairly sizeable group of English and Welsh bishops, including his predecessor at Hexham and Newcastle, Séamus Cunnningham, on their *ad limina* visit to Rome. They were received by Pope Francis, as a group, on 28 September. I have mentioned above that when Byrne and the other bishops asked the Holy Father for a message to take back to their dioceses, the Pope said the matter was simple: we are to live our faith with joy. Joy was his great emphasis.[3]

On 4 February 2019, Pope Francis appointed Byrne as Bishop of Hexham and Newcastle. Bishop Byrne moved from Birmingham to Newcastle on 20 March 2019, St Cuthbert's Day, and he was installed in Newcastle Cathedral, on 25 March, by the Archbishop of Liverpool, Malcolm McMahon OP, assisted by Bishop Séamus Cunningham. The Apostolic Nuncio, Archbishop Edward Adams, Cardinal Vincent Nichols and many other bishops and priests were also present. Byrne took the episcopal motto *soli Deo*, "to or for God alone", commenting that in the final analysis it is only God that really matters.

In his homily at the Mass, Bishop Byrne acknowledged the very early beginning of the diocese and recognized himself as a successor of St Cuthbert. He went on to say:

> As for any bishop it is my responsibility to accompany you on this journey. Firstly, by helping you hold firm to the Gospel which is handed on to us by the apostles and taught by the Church; we proclaim its truth in season and out. It is also my responsibility to help sanctify and help build up the Church in this diocese, especially by my care and leadership of the priests and people. Of course, the Church does not exist in a vacuum. All of us are called to be missionary and to reach out to those who have not heard the Gospel, to the poor and marginalised for whatever reason. I look forward to working with our fellow Christians and other faith groups to contribute to the common good in our region. All of this is a great task and can only be done with you and assisted

by your prayer. Cardinal Hume (a great son of Newcastle!) once famously said that the bishops are buoyed up by the prayers of the faithful. I ask your prayers today.

Bishop Byrne courted some controversy early on as bishop when the diocese sold the Grade I-listed East Denton Hall, in the west end of the city, that had been the bishop's residence since the Second World War, and bought a new property in West Avenue, Gosforth. It has been described in the press as a stunning, recently refurbished, six-bedroom property with en suite bathrooms, a sun terrace and a gym. Following Bishop Byrne's commitment to the poor of the diocese, some questioned whether this was entirely appropriate, especially in the light of Pope Francis' endorsement of simple living, and his rejection of the papal apartments. However, it should be observed that Bishop Byrne himself had no part in the decision of the diocesan trustees, who insisted that the bishop's new house and office was cheaper to run than the previous property, which is some 400 years old.[4] We may observe in passing that Bishop Kieran Conry, the fourth Bishop of Arundel and Brighton, similarly sold the historic bishop's house at Storrington when the upkeep became unduly expensive, replacing it with a cheaper property at Pease Pottage in Surrey.

Notes

[1] Meriol Trevor, *Newman's Journey* (Glasgow: Collins, 1974), p. 124.
[2] See *The Sower*, Birmingham archdiocesan magazine, Advent 2018.
[3] Ibid.
[4] See *Newcastle Chronicle*, 1 November 2020.

Epilogue

The Catechism of the Catholic Church teaches that the role or task of the bishops, who have the fullness of the sacrament of Holy Orders, is to teach, sanctify and govern. Similarly, St Gregory in his famous rule for bishops (*Regula Pastoralis* of c. 590) taught that a bishop is to be a teacher and physician of souls. He is to preach, reprove, rebuke and exhort, by precept and example, guiding all souls to salvation. Without wanting to judge, we may say that these criteria do provide a fitting framework to assess, or better characterize, the bishops of Hexham and Newcastle. What were their respective strengths and weaknesses? Or to ask the same question in a slightly different way, what do they have in common and what are the differences between them?

It is fascinating to me that fourteen bishops and two auxiliaries who were all called or appointed to the same task, to teach, sanctify and govern their diocese, could approach and execute that task in such a variety of ways. Sir Anthony Seldon, former vice-chancellor of the University of Buckingham and historian, recently presented a series of radio programmes marking 300 years of British prime ministers, from Sir Robert Walpole to Boris Johnson. I was struck forcibly by the sheer variety of personalities and personal stories behind a group of people ostensibly all doing the "same job", and it is not dissimilar with the bishops.

Some were great builders of the diocese: Hogarth, obviously, the first bishop established the new diocese(s), organizing parishes and clergy, establishing churches and setting the diocese that we see today in motion. Chadwick too developed and continued this work and invited many religious congregations to the diocese, following his extensive review in the late 1860s. Bishop Thorman similarly did much to rebuild the diocese after the First World War, establishing new churches and church schools.

His successor Joseph McCormack had the same task, although arguably an even bigger one, after the ravages of the Second World War.

Many of the bishops had a particular interest in education, founding and nurturing Catholic schools. Bishop Hogarth again recognized education as a way out of poverty and founded St Augustine's Primary School in Darlington. His successor Chadwick opened St Cuthbert's Grammar School in Newcastle, which was further developed and supported by Bishop Bewick who, as I have said, maintained rooms at the school for his use. In the twentieth century, Bishop McCormack worked tirelessly to further the causes of Catholic education and defended the right of the Church to educate its own in the faith. Bishop Séamus Cunningham studied religious education and catechesis in Bayswater and handed on the fruits of his labours in the diocese in the late 1970s.

Many of the bishops were notable scholars. Chadwick, Bewick, O'Callaghan and Preston were all doctors of divinity, and Bewick in particular was regarded as a brilliant Latin scholar. Bishop Swindlehurst was exceptional in holding three pontifical licences in philosophy, theology and canon law, and Griffiths was distinguished by his first in chemistry from Oxford: not an insignificant achievement in 1950 when first-class degrees were awarded significantly less often than they are now.

A number of the bishops are particularly noted for their pastoral zeal. Bishop Thorman, at one time an orphan, established social provisions for the Catholic children of the diocese and founded the Children's Care and Homes Committee. He was also involved in the work of the Catholic Guild and served as its president. Bishops Griffiths, who was given the sobriquet "bishop for the young", established the Youth Ministry Team and was involved in visits to papal World Youth Days. Bishop Dunn similarly involved himself particularly with the youth of the diocese, as well as previously having found himself in a frontline pastoral position during the Handsworth riots of the mid-1980s. Bishop Byrne is noted for his lifelong commitment to ministry to those in prison.

Finally, two of the bishops seem to me to inhabit categories of their own. Bishop Wilkinson retired from ministry on account of his poor health and on his doctor's orders. He retired to a farm and bred cattle, surely an experience not shared by many prelates! But as we have seen he was subsequently appointed the fifth Bishop of Hexham and Newcastle, a position he held for twenty years. Even more remarkably, he was, at the same time, president or rector of Ushaw. His request to Cardinal Vaughan that he might be allowed to resign from his duties at the age of seventy was clearly a heartfelt plea. Wilkinson was not a scholar particularly, despite his position at Ushaw, but was undoubtedly a formidable administrator, applying the lessons he had learnt on his farm to the efficient running of seminary and diocese.

Bishop O'Callaghan too can best be described as *sui generis*. Recall that he was an Oblate of St Charles and had successfully steered the Venerable English College in Rome through some turbulent times while rector there in the late nineteenth century. He was raised to the purple by way of a reward for his labours, but this was a reward he didn't want and for which he was entirely unsuited. He accepted the preferment out of a sense of duty, but significantly his episcopal ordination had to be postponed when he was overcome by anxiety. Furthermore, after many years in Rome, O'Callaghan struggled to recognize the attractions of the North-East, particularly its climate! O'Callaghan was swift to appoint an episcopal vicar, who soon became his auxiliary bishop, and he resigned the see within two years of his appointment. This could be seen as dereliction of duty, but I think that would be uncharitable and I prefer to think that O'Callaghan was brave to recognize his own limits, and when he realized the task was beyond him, he nobly stood down to make way for another. He is the only bishop of Hexham and Newcastle buried outside the UK, and the only one who was raised to the rank of archbishop.

These then, and others, are the men who have steered and guided the Petrine barque in Hexham and Newcastle over the last 170 or so years. The story, as I have presented it, is incomplete as I have not been able to include every detail, and as soon as it is finished it starts to go out of date as history unfolds. But the record of history is ever thus, necessarily partial and always a part of a larger work in progress: so I present this work as a contribution, a summary of the work of a group of significant men, whose ministry may be traced back to Oswald, Aidan and Cuthbert in the seventh century and whose successors will extend into the indeterminacy of the future.

Acknowledgements

I am most grateful to Dr Ray Davies, who assisted with some of the genealogical research in this text and generously read it through, making many helpful corrections and suggestions for improvement. I am, of course, grateful to all the staff at Sacristy Press.

Bibliography

Anstruther, G., *The Seminary Priests*, Vol. I (Gateshead: Northumberland Press, 1968).

Brady, W. M., *Annals of the Catholic Hierarchy in England and Scotland AD 1585–1876* (London: John Mozley Stark, 1883).

Dwyer, G., *Diocese of Portsmouth—Past and Present* (Portsmouth: Portsmouth Diocesan Centenary Committee, 1981).

Flannery OP, A., *Vatican Council II: The Conciliar and Postconciliar Documents*, Vol. I (New York: Costello Publishing, 1975, 1996).

Gard, R., "The Archives of the Diocese of Hexham and Newcastle", *Catholic Archives*, 19 (1999), pp. 24–41.

Gard, R. "Societies II", *Catholic Archives*, 22 (2002), pp. 26–34.

Gilley, S., "The Legacy of William Hogarth 1786–1866", *Recusant History*, 25:2 (2000), pp. 249–62.

Gooch, L., "Thomas William Wilkinson (1825–1909), Bishop of Hexham and Newcastle upon Tyne (1889–1909)", *Northern Catholic History*, 13 (1981).

Gooch, L., *From Jacobite to Radical: The Catholics of North East England, 1688–1850* (Durham University Ph.D. thesis, 1989).

Hart, C., *The Early Story of St Cuthbert's Grammar School* (London: Burns & Oates, 1941).

Hayward, T. C., "College Rectors–VIII", *The Venerabile* XVI:4 (1954), pp. 215–31.

Heenan, John, *A Crown of Thorns* (London: Hodder and Stoughton, 1974).

Hoegemann, B., "Newman and Rome", in Philippe Lefebvre and Colin Mason (eds), *John Henry Newman in His Time*, (Oxford: Family Publications, 2007), pp. 61–81.

Jennings, P. (ed.), *Benedict XVI and Blessed John Henry Newman: The State Visit 2010, the Official Record* (London: CTS, 2010).

Kenny, A., *A Path from Rome* (London: Sidgwick and Jackson, 1985).
Larsen, C., *Catholic Bishops of Great Britain* (Durham: Sacristy Press, 2016).
Longley, C., *The Worlock Archive* (London: Geoffrey Chapman, 2000).
MacDonald LCM, A., *In the Footsteps of Venerable Mary Potter, 1882-1913* (London: LCM, 2005).
Milburn, D., *A History of Ushaw College* (Ushaw: 1964).
Murphy-O'Connor, C., *An English Spring* (London: Bloomsbury, 2015).
Newcastle City Council, "Notable dates connected with Newcastle during WW 2: Local Studies Factsheet no. 4" (Newcastle Local Studies and Family History Centre, 2009).
Parry, D. (trans. and ed.), *The Rule of St Benedict* (London: DLT, 1984).
Phillips, F., *Bishop Beck and English Education 1949-1959* (Lampeter: Edward Mellin Press, 1990).
Pickering, Fr A., *Our Lady and St Oswin, Tynemouth and Cullercoats: Story of Our Parish* (Tynemouth, 1990).
Plumb, B., *Arundel to Zabi: A Biographical Dictionary of the Catholic Bishops of England and Wales (Deceased) 1623-2000* (Wigan: North West Catholic History Society, 1987, 2006).
Pollen, J. H., *Acts of the English Martyrs Hitherto Unpublished* (London: Burns & Oates, 1891).
Pope John XXIII, *Journal of a Soul*, trans. Dorothy White (London: Geoffrey Chapman, 1965).
Power, S. B., *The development of Roman Catholic education in the nineteenth century, with some reference to the diocese of Hexham and Newcastle* (Durham University, MA dissertation, 2003).
Russell, David R., *History written for St Edward's Centenary Celebrations, 23 October 2011*, <http://www.northtynesidecatholic.org.uk/wp-content/uploads/2015/02/St-Edwards-History1.pdf>, accessed 2 November 2021.
Stapleton, J. (ed.), *The A&B Story 1965-1990: The First Twenty-Five Years* (Diocese of Arundel and Brighton, 1990).

Sterling, T. R., *St Patrick's RC Church, Felling 1895–2014* (2014), <http://www.stpatricks-felling.co.uk/wp-content/uploads/The-history-of-St-Patricks-Booklet-1.pdf>, accessed 2 November 2021.

Tanner, N., *New Short History of the Catholic Church* (London: Burns & Oates, 2011).

Trevor, M., *Newman's Journey* (Glasgow: Collins, 1974).

Walsh, M. J., *The Westminster Cardinals* (London: Burns & Oates, 2008).

Wild, G., *The Darlington Catholics* (Darlington: Carmel Convent, 1993).

Williams, M., *The Venerable English College Rome* (Leominster: Gracewing, 1979, 2008).

Williams, M., *Oscott College in the Twentieth Century* (Leominster: Gracewing, 2001).

EU GPSR Authorized Representative:

LOGOS EUROPE, 9 rue Nicolas Poussin, 17000 La Rochelle, France

contact@logoseurope.eu

www.ingramcontent.com/pod-product-compliance
Lightning Source LLC
Chambersburg PA
CBHW071435160426
43195CB00013B/1912